D0745841

Benjamin Banneker

Benjamin Banneker. (Library of Congress collection)

Benjamin Banneker

Surveyor, Astronomer, Publisher, Patriot

Charles Cerami

John Wiley & Sons, Inc.

ISBN: 0-471-38752-5

10 9 8 7 6 5 4 3 2 1

to my long-time and valued friend
James C. (Jimmy) Littlejohn

Contents

Preface

Why, I had long wondered, was the name of Benjamin Banneker so little known? For a black man of the late eighteenth century to have had a leading role in surveying the new capital city of Washington, D.C., surely was a feat to recall and celebrate. Yet even in Washington, his name on one school building is the main memorial—and its students have no idea who he was.

When I began learning more about this brilliant man, I was astonished to find that the Washington survey was far from his chief accomplishment, a revelation that deepened the mystery of his relative obscurity. One of the finest minds of the age and surely one of the greatest untutored scientists of all time has been passed over with minimal attention. Only after researching Banneker's contacts with the Founding Fathers and their reactions to this African American did I realize that his rare talents and sterling character were quite consciously obscured by his white "colleagues." Having become dependent on him without knowing his race, they clearly feared the political backlash if Southern leaders suspected a move to demonstrate that blacks were capable of more than manual labor and should not be considered mere chattel. It would be misleading to say that there was a "cover-up" in the modern sense, but with the limited press coverage of that time, the lack of even minimal recognition accomplished much the same result.

The man we meet here was actually the mental superior when he found himself among the Founding Fathers. Most of them were brilliant men and some multifaceted, but unlike Banneker, they were not geniuses with the rare innate ability to discover truths for themselves and then make them seem obvious to others. Among the founders, only Benjamin Franklin was on that level, but he was older than the others and died at about the time Banneker moved beyond his tobacco farm.

In a perfect world, the subject of race would occupy no more than a single line in this book, like a description of height or weight. It would be simply the biography of a great scientist. But if that were the case, he would have been world-famous for two centuries and the subject of many biographies. The insights he had—with hardly any education or equipment—make it likely that adequate schooling and a normal place in society would have enabled him to accelerate the history of astronomy itself. But in the real world, it would be incomplete and unfair to assess Banneker's deep wisdom and his accomplishments as scientist, philosopher, and publisher without recognizing that all this was done while scratching out a living as a tobacco farmer and thinking himself lucky to be a free black. As a personal accomplishment, Benjamin Banneker's life story surpasses the careers of later scientists whose image of the cosmos was formed among brilliant colleagues in the world's great universities. And perhaps it is a greater lesson in living for all, a sharper perspective on the distorting role of ethnic background.

From the time he was five, it had been obvious that young Benjamin had a remarkable mind. With little or no formal schooling, he made the most of help from his loving grandparents and books borrowed from a Quaker teacher to achieve an elegant writing style and an acquaintance with the classics. But it was in science that he truly excelled. Even before he had help of any kind, he was fascinated by astronomy and developed some amazing intuitions. When he finally had access to a telescope and two books on the subject, he reached independent conclusions far in advance of his time. On his own, too, he mastered such science-oriented skills as watchmaking and surveying—which made him ready to assist in the planning of Washington, D.C., when the call came.

Today, when every difference of origin or complexion puts us on the shaking tightrope of race, it requires a mental feat to imagine how a mind with such cosmic interests saw itself in a frozen world where blacks were supposed to behave deferentially. His own ancestry was probably the most unusual in the history of this country. For sixty years, he lived a divided life, doing his expected duty as a freeborn farmer on his own acreage while thinking great thoughts in his off-hours. Through a few patrician neighbors who could share his scientific interests, he had one foot in the white world, often as the leader in solving any technical problem they discussed. He probably had at least three sharp encounters with the kind of terror that could strike a black person at any moment. One of these may have involved his only adventure in love and a tragic ending, although I question the truth of that story. Because these incidents were spread over an otherwise tranquil lifetime, even friends and neighbors thought he lived an exceptionally peaceful life. Indeed, for those first six decades, he was outwardly little affected by the horrors his enslaved black brethren were experiencing.

Then, when he had come to know Thomas Jefferson personally, Banneker struck. To the author of the Declaration of Independence, he wrote a blistering letter that can stand with it proudly in reasoning and style—similarly audacious, courageous, and potentially explosive. The mores of early American society were at least civil enough to make Secretary of State Jefferson refrain from punishing Banneker for the raging insult. He hushed it up instead. It was more than half a century before the great black leaders we have come to know as pioneers of civil rights began to make themselves heard. But Banneker had taken the first risk—and the greatest, because he could not know how Secretary Jefferson and the whole white world might react.

The fact that other, more venomous enemies burned down the scientist's cabin and all his papers at the moment of his funeral makes it daunting to attempt a full and responsible biography. The lost journals of his youthful years would have helped to pierce the obscurity that cloaked all black persons in that day. As it is, the series of early snapshots we are able to see helps to intensify his emergence as a vibrant person when all his gifts come into view. Indeed, many white persons became great admirers and sought him out for his wise counsel. The challenge of making this most remarkable early American known to today's more enlightened readership is exhilarating. And the fact that his life ran a course opposite that of most human stories, gathering force and joy as he grew older, adds to the pleasure of describing it.

Acknowledgments

Well beyond the usual *pro forma* bow to one's editor, I have been struck by Hana Umlauf Lane's rare ability to note the smallest details while also relating every sentence to an overall plan. Not many editors read with such interest that they can pencil a reminder on a late page, saying, "Slightly repetitious?—see Chapter 2." I am tired, but very grateful. Hana surely joins me in gratitude to my friend and agent, Bob Silverstein. He is truly a collaborator who frequently drives me into rewriting before the editors do, and we all benefit from his judgment.

While every person or organization shown in my list of sources was genuinely helpful to me, and some of the libraries named are much larger, I want to single out the Howard County (Maryland) Historical Society for the special interest shown by its librarians and even some of its members who came forward to suggest new places to look.

It was less of a surprise, because of long experience, to find that the Washingtoniana Room of the Martin Luther King Memorial Library in Washington, D.C., gave generous personal attention and brought forth old books and papers of great interest.

Of all the persons I talked with, Sam Hopkins made me feel most as if I were spending hours in the eighteenth century. And Ann Ryder, with fingers on the pulses of Ellicott City and Howard County, repeatedly pointed me in new directions.

1

The Prince
and the Convict

The hunt for ancestral talent or character that might explain the birth of a genius is usually futile. In the case of Benjamin Banneker, however, it has intriguing aspects that refuse to be ignored. It is as though God were saying "Stir and mix my people as you will, some of each new generation will try to follow old paths, a few will seek new ways, and in every ten million there will be one who astonishes you."

As a young woman, Banneker's maternal grandmother, Molly Welsh, worked as a dairymaid for a great family near Devon, England. Hers was a hard, unbending master who moved to punish the girl to the full extent of the law when, one day in 1682, she spilled an entire pail of milk. He refused to believe her stammered excuse that the cow had moved suddenly and made her jump. No, the master insisted, the evidence did not show that any such accident had occurred. She had clearly stolen and probably sold the milk, he claimed. He turned her over to the constabulary for prosecution, knowing that a guilty verdict for any theft could result in the death penalty. Even if this enterprising young woman had actually been selling a little milk on the side, the prescribed sentence would now seem unthinkable.

The court paid no more attention to Molly's protestations than her master had, and she was pronounced guilty. But before giving the sentence of death, the judge turned to a provision of the law that could moderate the judgment. If the convict could read (presumably showing a little more excuse for existence), the punishment could be reduced to forced "emigration," meaning shipment to one of England's colonies where the miscreant could spend a certain number of years of unpaid servitude with a colonist. So the order to "Bring the Book!" was given, the Bible was put before Molly Welsh, and she read it with a flourish, for she was a religious girl and a daily reader of the Good Book.

A sentence of seven years' servitude in the Maryland colony was pronounced. Many Marylanders of that day deeply resented the use of their beautiful area as a penal colony. The idea that seven years in Maryland was considered an appropriate alternative to death by hanging was a sort of sick joke at the time. To the life-loving Molly, it was a blessed escape, and she sailed off determined to make the most of her new existence. She landed at the port of Annapolis (which was then called Providence) in 1683.

There is no record of who became her master in this new world. He had to pay the price of her passage, and in return, he bought seven years of her life. It is clear that he was a tobacco planter, as most of the area's farmers were. Some historians feel that he must have been one of the Quakers who were infusing a greater spirit of justice into the colony. In any case, Molly was undoubtedly fortunate in finding a fair-minded employer, for her spirit was unbroken and her health good when the term was finished. Also, this master was punctilious in fulfilling his duty to give the released convict everything required by the remarkably detailed rules ordained in the law: a specific number of blouses, skirts, shoes, and other pieces of apparel, an ox, a hoe, a gun, fifty acres of arable farmland, and a small amount of cash to make a new start as a farmer. The law, in short, was rather enlightened in providing for an ex-convict to become a future colonist. But if that person was a woman with no help, the transition was, nevertheless, arduous.

⁓

With her new belongings in hand, Molly reached her property, land worth only a dollar or two per acre in that day, situated on the northern side of the Patapsco River, the substantial west-east waterway that flows fifty-two miles, right past Baltimore, and empties from its wide mouth into the Atlantic Ocean. Her small farm was far upland from the more valuable riverfront, and on a slight slope. But with just a few tree stumps, it was land that could be made productive. As an experienced farm worker, she would have had more than a little notion of what needed to be done, but also would have known that she alone could not accomplish it. For the construction of a shelter had first priority, and that was beyond her abilities. The next steps— the preparation of the land and the planting of a crop—all would have needed at least one man, preferably two, to do the heaviest work.

The feistiness and determination of this young woman, well into her twenties by this time, are already clear. Now she demonstrated a degree of ingenuity far beyond the ordinary. As her own story has been handed down through generations of neighbor families, Molly first arranged to stay with her old employer a little longer in order to avoid sleeping out in the elements. But one morning, after hearing that an incoming slave ship had docked, she rose and went to the nearby harbor. There, with burly colonists all around her, this diminutive woman who had so recently achieved respectability joined in looking over the black men who were being offered for sale. With a decisiveness that was to be a lifelong trait, Molly settled on two whom she thought would do. One was a plain-looking, brawny man who struck her as friendly and trainable. The other was tall and lean, almost disinterestedly looking down on the colonists who stared at him. It was hard to imagine him as a farmhand, but she was somehow reluctant to leave him behind. Because he was priced lower than her first choice—apparently the other colonists didn't see him as a good worker, either—she was able to buy both of them out of the cash her master had given her, leaving dangerously little for building materials, tools, and food to live on until a salable crop could be raised.

Other accounts of this transaction that have passed down over the generations are slightly different. One suggests that free land was not normally part of an indentured servant's exit package and that Molly had to rent land from a neighboring farmer, paying from the proceeds of her crops until she could buy her own land. Other historians also believe that the high cost of good young slaves would have made such a purchase impossible unless Molly somehow had more money than the usual payoff from her former master. Perhaps she had penuriously saved cash that she had earned by working extra hours during those seven years. Or she might have won her employer's trust enough to get a loan for these starting expenses. Whichever version is accurate, it underscores the firmness of her character and the saving ways that later helped build her family.

As she turned to farming with her two slaves, Molly soon discovered that her judgment of the two helpers had been exactly right. The heavier man was very good-natured, a willing worker, and amazingly sanguine about making far more effort than the other. Although her words meant nothing to him, he strained cheerfully to understand and respond to her pantomime signals. When Molly grew exasperated that her other choice often lay on the ground, propped on an elbow, watching while the heavy labor went on, the one who bore the brunt of this lassitude managed, with facial expressions and hand gestures, to make her realize that the reclining man was not supposed to work because he was the son of a king. She came to understand that "Banneka," as he called himself, was the eldest son, destined to succeed his father until he was captured in an enemy raid and sold to slave traders. (Some scholars believe that his given name was simply Banne and that Ka was a family name.) And while Banneka's dignity made him less eager to engage in pantomime communication, a special understanding developed between him and Molly. People forced to live and work together in such circumstances very often invent a simple private language in a remarkably short time, with each quickly learning the relatively few words that the other uses repeatedly. Just such a blending of sounds and cultures, stirred by sheer necessity, must have made this trio of castaways into a viable little community within weeks.

In time, this tale took a romantic turn, and here the historical evidence is firm. As soon as the small farm was established— a matter of several years—Molly gave Banneka his papers as a freed man, and married him. Nothing is known of their courtship or which one of them proposed to the other, but there are enough hard facts to establish that they were married and had four daughters. A favorite one, called Mary, was probably the second child and was born in 1700. They were a remarkably devoted couple until Banneka's death before age fifty. Molly referred to him as "The Prince," and the family always called her "Big Ma-Ma."

Although her husband's aversion to work had remained a constant, Molly understood that it might have been linked to a serious physical reason, for Banneka had never fully recovered from the inhuman conditions of the slave ship nor adapted to the winter months in Maryland. In any case, while he lived he more than made up for his laboring lapses by using certain higher skills that a chief's son would have learned in order to lead his people in the harsh African environment. One was a great hunting ability, which enabled him to return from forays with meats of inestimable value in the early lean years. Even more striking, after tobacco was selected as the crop of choice, was Banneka's astonishing ability to foretell the weather. The neighboring farmers came to look enviously at the way this family always seemed to plant its heaviest crop when there was going to be fine weather and to cut back when conditions turned out to be less favorable. It was even said that Banneka foretold the direction of prevailing winds long enough in advance to locate his plantings with uncanny precision. He was inventive, too; he devised a way of channeling water from a small spring to parts of their acreage, and this irrigation made the farm flourish in a way that none of the surrounding properties could match.

Such skills are of interest because of their probable link with the astronomical intuitions and clever craftsmanship that his grandson would have. They also shed some light on a question that has never been definitively answered: Exactly where in Africa did Banneka come from?

It is important to avoid the Euro-American tendency to see Africa's people as an undifferentiated mass with skin color as a chief characteristic. Africa's communities are every bit as diverse as those of the Western world, and each unwilling immigrant who came to America in chains was at least partly shaped by his or her place of birth and tribal upbringing. In Banneka's case, some authorities believe he was a native of Senegal, with one of his parents having been from the Wolof tribe and the other from the Fulani. That view deserves respect, but there are stronger reasons to think Banneka's lineage traces to an area adjacent to Guinea now known as Mali. And while there are several distinct peoples within Mali's present boundaries, it is likely that one small group called the Dogon (now numbering about 200,000) are Banneka's ancestors. That would not rule out the possibility that his mother was, indeed, a Fulani, as that tribe also extended into the territory of present-day Mali and has had a long relationship with the Dogon.

It is a distinguished and intriguing heritage. For one thing, it has long been said that the Dogon people, many centuries ago, charted the stars with astonishing accuracy. Whether this is truth or myth is a subject of controversy among researchers, but there is no doubt at all about the superior skills of the Dogon in other technical fields, especially irrigation and farming. The fact that precisely these talents underlay Banneka's success in Maryland and were passed on to a descendant must be considered as much more than coincidence, for numerous other Dogon characteristics and character traits are detectable in what is known of Banneka and then equally pronounced in the talents of Banneka's remarkable grandson. The Dogon's absorption with the cosmos and with numerology, their reserved manner and dedication to work, and their pleasantly nonconfrontational manner—all exactly foreshadow the interests and manner that Banneka passed along to the descendant who indirectly inherited his teachings.

After his capture, the two likeliest places that Banneka would have passed through on his way to America are an old fort along the coast of present-day Ghana or another of the infamous "slave castles" on Gorée Island, off the shores of Senegal. The conditions were such that some forty million people are

Stowing the cargo on a slaver at night. Believed to be from a mid-nineteenth-century book showing slaves being packed into place for the night, with the pretense that each is positioned on his or her right side for health reasons. (Library of Congress collection)

believed to have died in captivity over more than three centuries. To endure that and the added horror of crossing the ocean on a slave ship left many of the survivors physically maimed or blighted by disease, and Banneka was clearly one of these victims, never fully well again and destined to have a foreshortened life.

History doesn't tell us how this mixed marriage almost three hundred years ago was perceived. It is no cause for surprise that Molly had no prejudice against such a match, for her own harrowing experiences would have made her realize what unfair judgments and punishments blacks had to endure. But was the marriage frowned on by other Marylanders? Was it

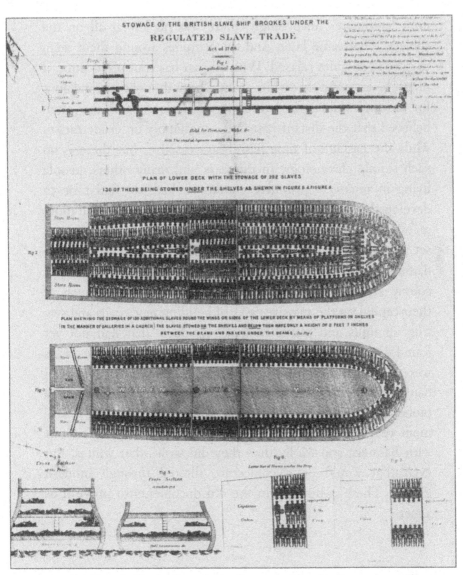

An official British plan for slave stowage. Some consider this the most appalling picture of human savagery ever made, for it is not an artist's imagining, but a government document, indicating that this represents a humane move to reduce total cargo on this ship from 600 slaves to a maximum of 454 slaves. Even this impression of sardines in a can fails to capture the horror inflicted on some slaves by placing them on shelves with little air space. (Library of Congress collection)

even legitimate? Surprisingly, there was no law at all on the subject. That came later. And the attitudes around them seem to have been quite relaxed. With all that has transpired since, it might be assumed that whites would have thought it scandalous for a white woman to have married a slave. It is too often believed that the distant past had a monopoly on crude racism while the passage of time has always eased it, but there is no such simple chronology. In this case and many others, people living in relatively primitive conditions had not had time to develop the many prejudices that grew when life became more secure. While The Prince and Big Ma-Ma were struggling to set up a viable way to live, their neighbors were occupied with daunting problems of their own. Even the officials who ran the colony and the wealthiest landowners were risking much of their capital on the massive tasks of building new roads and setting up mills and plants to make products that had not yet found a market. Fires that wiped out such uninsurable assets were common; unforeseen competition that created sudden bankruptcies cropped up over and over. Every person was a pioneer, and pioneers set up social rules mainly in their retirement years. It is likely that white neighbors had less contact with Banneka and Molly than they did with other whites. But even that would be a conjecture filtered through modern glasses. There is nothing in the old documents to prove it as a fact.

When the couple's daughter Mary reached a marriageable age, she was a tall, copper-toned beauty. To marry her to a slave from a nearby farm was flatly ruled out, for the law had tightened, and anyone who made such a marriage was automatically condemned to slavery, too. One popular account has it that her mother, Molly, used her own old method to procure a suitable husband who could be freed before marriage. Together, they supposedly went to meet an incoming slave ship, looked over the newcomers, and made another life-altering decision. They are said to have bought a young slave who seemed alert, sensible, and gave a sign of pleasure on seeing Mary.

An alternate version seems likelier. The young man had arrived on a slave ship some years earlier, was bought by a colonist, and proved to be fiercely independent. He escaped twice, and may have lived with Indians for a time. But then he had the good fortune to be sold to an unusual planter who admired the slave's spirit and was especially impressed by his desire to be baptized a Christian. He felt that this man had too much dignity to be a slave, and he freed him.

The young man's pleasure at the sight of Mary, at least, must be counted as a very accurate part of either account, for despite his independent spirit, he gladly accepted the name Robert Bannaky and became another vital part of this family who demonstrated character and ability that few in the white world thought these unwilling arrivals from Africa possessed. Robert Banneky's character was such to raise the question of how many other African Americans might have emulated the successful career paths of immigrants from Europe if they had found a reasonable amount of respect in America, rather than the numbing embrace of slavery.

Not only was Robert to become a fine father to his four children with Mary, but he also managed the farm superbly. As he prospered, he bought a twenty-five-acre nearby farm, naming it Timber Poynt. While Mary, widely admired as a lady of great beauty, was also becoming well known in the area for special skills with herbal medicines, Robert helped Molly to save and reinvest so well that their combined landholdings eventually quadrupled.

On November 9, 1731, Robert and Mary had a son whom they named Benjamin. Those inclined to see mystical or divine patterns in historical happenings have pointed out that this man who may have been the rarest human being born in that year happened to come into a colony that was surpassing its neighbors in making steps toward a new spirit of freedom and compassion. Although the intellect of Benjamin Banneker would have been a great one regardless of his birthplace, he might have groped in vain anywhere else for ways to satisfy his great thirst for knowledge. He might never have found the conditions to facilitate his self-education or the neighbors who would recognize his qualification for a high place in the world if Maryland had not had some startling early champions of egalitarianism.

In 1634, Lord Baltimore, a man who never crossed the ocean to visit his American properties, had made Maryland the first colony to have full religious freedom. A Religious Toleration Act was adopted in 1649, although it was blighted by years of anti-Catholic laws dictated from Britain. Puritans and Quakers began moving to Maryland to escape the insistence on conformity in other colonies. A most important move came in 1660, when a tightening of religious laws in Virginia caused three hundred Quakers to move to Maryland. Following up on this, Quaker leaders from England, including the Society's founder, George Fox, visited Maryland in the 1670s and began to preach about the inconsistency of slaveholding by people who professed to be Christians. In 1688, five years after Molly Welsh's arrival as a convict, Quakers who had emigrated from Germany made the first written protest against slavery the American colonies had ever seen. And in the early part of the eighteenth century, State Senator Charles Carroll, brother of the Jesuit who founded Georgetown University, proposed a law

Cecil Calvert, the second Lord Baltimore, shown with his grandson and holding a map of the Maryland Colony. Although he never crossed the Atlantic to visit the great property he governed, his relatively enlightened rule made this colony a place where Benjamin Banneker's father could buy his own land and see his son gain more respect than most other Southern colonies would have allowed. (Enoch Pratt Free Library, Baltimore, Maryland)

to abolish slavery in Maryland. It lost by a vote of 35 to 20, but considering the fact that large slave owners had a disproportionate voting power, a one-man-one-vote count would have made it a winner; in other words, a growing sentiment among the people for abolition of slavery was clear.

"All these steps, culminating in a time when Benjamin Banneker would be pointed to as an example of the African-American's mental abilities, formed a very real part of the movement that brought about the Declaration of Independence," says Samuel Hopkins,* a Maryland historian whose own family has multiple links to the subject of social justice. "The American people did not go to war just because of tea and taxes. They were trying to form a new society that gave people far more freedom from harsh control. Molly Welsh went from an England that nearly executed her for spilling milk to a colony that gave her a second chance. And while it was no Garden of Eden even for free black persons, it was moving toward a time when Benjamin Banneker's role was to have great significance."

This analysis is supported by numerous modern social and anthropological observations on how progressive changes in communities come about. While the changes are usually pioneered by a handful of independent thinkers who seem out of step at first, these risk-takers may flourish when a critical mass of people around them begins to relax its opposition to the changes and then makes hesitant moves to adopt the new political correctness.

Much as he was loved by his parents, young Benjamin was given even more attention by his grandmother. She made the

---

* Hopkins is a descendant of the Senator Carroll named here and also a great-nephew of Johns Hopkins, who founded Baltimore's renowned medical institution. But nothing in his lineage seems as significant to him as his direct descent from George Ellicott, who became Banneker's closest white friend and scientific collaborator.

amazingly bright boy her first interest in life. Although local lore has long held that Benjamin, as a young boy, acquired a great deal of wisdom from his grandfather Banneka, a study of the calendar shows that this pleasant story could not have involved a face-to-face meeting between the two. Banneka must have been born in 1672 or earlier in order to seem an attractive young man to the older Molly when she bought him in 1690. He would therefore have been at least fifty-nine years old when his grandson Benjamin was born in 1731 (which is a verified date). But every recollection and book, including an unquestioned contemporary account, says that the grandfather died before age fifty. So there is no way young Benjamin could have known his grandfather.

It is a fact, however, that Benjamin knew farm methods, weather wisdom, and astronomical facts that appear to have come from the Dogon. These remarkable Africans had—and have to this day—thoughts that astonish their neighbors in Mali and occasionally others of the wider world. Some of Benjamin's Dogon ways were probably inherited traits, but much of the lore had to be learned by word of mouth. His father, Robert, was not a Dogon. So it must be that grandmother Molly, who had such respect for Banneka's princely background, had listened to her husband's words so carefully that she could pass on this kind of information to her adored grandson. After all, Molly herself had done much of the actual farming work in earlier days. It was not as though she had been a pampered woman with no thought of men's subjects. From the time she married, she had firmly embraced the black side of her family as her own. So it now appears clear that this astonishing woman— who had begun life as a lowly milkmaid—could not only give Benjamin a grounding in good English and fine handwriting, but was equally able to pass along African wisdom that he never turned away from, even when he learned more modern science.

Molly must often have recalled the day the Bible had saved her life when she used the same book as a manual of literacy for little Benjamin. Yet it did not make him quick to join any organized religion when he was grown. On that subject, he would always have a mind of his own. But by learning to read the Old and New Testaments and even memorizing biblical passages at a remarkably young age, he came to develop the style of speech and even of writing that gave him an ability to communicate on a level far beyond that of a simple tobacco farmer.

When Benjamin was six, in 1837, Robert Bannaky acquired a separate hundred-acre site not very far away from the original farm, bartering 7,000 pounds of tobacco to pay for it. For a time, he owned both Timber Poynt and this larger farm, called "Stout." The name of young Benjamin appears on the deed to that property, for his foresighted father wanted to be sure his firstborn would have a firm claim to it. Although they remained in close contact with Molly, this now became the site of the Bannaky family's new cabin, and other cabins were later added as each child became an adult. Benjamin would live in his cabin alone until his death.

Banneker's hometown has been given as Elkridge in most accounts. That is generally correct as an indication of the area. But research has now proved that both Molly's farm and the larger one where Banneker spent most of his life were in an unnamed area that was later incorporated as the tiny mill town of Oella only in 1808, after his death.

Today, all of these residences are gone, but they are to be rebuilt as part of a Banneker Memorial that already features a modern marble museum building behind an imposing stone gateway and drive. Walking over the site, one is surprised to find it an attractive piece of property on a high rise that overlooks much of the surrounding area. At first sight, it seems too desirable for a small farmer to have afforded, but in 1737, the climb was a hard one. The costlier land was far below, where the city life was centered and the riverside provided transportation facilities. As in most parts of the world, the poorer folk had to move uphill to do their farming and transporting under harder conditions. Tired muscles were a price the poor often paid for the better views they enjoyed.

~

Around the time of this move, when Benjamin was between five and six years old, the family and much of the neighborhood began to talk of him as a phenomenon. He was a quiet boy, showing no sign of wanting attention, most often walking rather than running or jumping. Even at that young age, he seemed to show a trait inherited from his grandfather, The Prince. Odd as it is to say about a small boy, he was dignified. He had a graceful, compact way of moving, and an engaging charm. His large bright eyes seemed to be seeing a wider landscape than others saw, and they had a glow of instant understanding whenever anyone spoke to him. His responses were those of an educated, courteous adult. Most of the nearby small farmers—some black, some white—were unlettered folk. To hear a small boy answer a question with a quotation from the Bible, to see him write with a flowing hand, made their mouths fall agape. But it was his total domination of numbers that made him seem a being apart. Even when he was six, they began to ask him to check their uncertain financial figures. And their astonishment grew when he not only sorted them out instantly, but could later talk from memory about each person's array of numbers. His sense of logical reasoning was so precise that everything seemed to fall into place in his mind. And his recall was photographic. He would never lose that trait to the day of his death.

So Benjamin Banneker grew up with the sense of being a special person, much as a Mozart or a Menuhin, also prodigies, might have felt during childhood. Amazingly, it seemed to give him a premature sense of responsibility, rather than a spoiled child's egotism. His care about the little hilltop community sounds much like the account of Chicago's beloved Cardinal Bernardin, whose sister recalled that at age five he seemed to feel that any neighbor family's loss or trouble was something he had to think about and try to heal.

Benjamin does not seem to have let this precocious role interfere with a healthy view of reality. His grandmother's steady attention was his main source of information for some years, but Molly was too tough-minded to give a child impractically grand thoughts. His lamented grandfather, far from forgotten, was summoned by Molly to give him occasional glimpses of how the skies and clouds and winds relate to life on earth, but those were things that he would save in a corner of his mind and use over the years as an intuitive base for weighing the scientific facts he would learn from books. His parents, Robert and Mary, were the main programmers, and their no-nonsense attitude toward what had to be done built an underlying foundation. No prodigy ever had wiser parents, for although they probably didn't know his thoughts, they respected the mind that produced them. They also made sure he knew that arithmetical skills and beautiful handwriting did not make tobacco grow or put food on the table. As he grew a little older, he went out digging and planting with his father, an African whose superb managerial skills Benjamin recognized as another of the family's crown jewels. Robert taught discipline by example, but Benjamin was never cowed or coerced. He could study and he could go to a quiet corner and think—but only after the necessities of survival had been completed. That sense of priorities would never vary.

2

Lessons, Precious
and Painful

The development of a home-schooled mind is totally different from the course that most educated individuals follow as they mature. For the normal child, daily attendance at a school, conversations with companions, and exchanges with teachers contribute bits of information that will coalesce almost imperceptibly into knowledge, attitudes, opinions. If the influences are generally good ones, the result is said to be a "well-rounded" mind.

It was much different for Benjamin. He knew that his mother and father laid down the rules, but Mary and Robert were so totally occupied with farm work and ways to earn a little extra cash that they could not act as educators. The main learning input was from Molly and from what she could pass along of Banneka's African wisdom, but neither with any academic education of the kind that Benjamin was clearly hungering for. Molly provided him with the simple, basic literacy and logic of the Western world. Banneka's thoughts gave the feel for nature that derived from his African heritage. Beyond that, the boy would have to find and open other doors for himself. After learning basic reading skills while very small, he had no plan of instruction beyond further study of Molly's Bible, for there was no other book in the house.

It is certain that he was constantly schooling himself about the workings of the world around him, for entries from a diary that he began to keep later show that such observations came to his mind almost effortlessly. But history has left scant evidence of how this proceeded when he was five, six, or seven years old. No milestones were put in place to record his development, no report cards left behind to mark progress as new semesters went by, no childhood letters to relatives exist to show the progress of his thoughts. Instead, changes were marked only by chance happenings that introduced a new influence into his life.

One early lesson involved Banneker's first experience with racist terrorism and the "street smarts" that could only be learned from surviving a real-life test. In this case, it was so searing that the emotion he underwent during a matter of moments apparently obscured his usual precision about dates. Here, for one of the few times in his life, the superhuman memory he had on most subjects blurred. When he mentioned this incident in later life, he could only refer to the date as "sometime during my childhood years." Most of the surrounding facts, such as the apparent age of siblings and the time of a separate event that occurred later, would point to about age eight.

Although young Benjamin had never realized it before, his parents and grandparents knew that blacks, even free blacks, were facing an increasingly terrifying situation. Because of the South's growing demand for workers, healthy black persons were being bought and sold for higher and higher prices. That was an open invitation to lawless ruffians to invent a lucrative racket. A few tough whites would band together, calling themselves patrollers and pretending to be legally empowered to catch runaway slaves. They were really bounty hunters, with no legal status beyond the fact that neither citizens nor authorities did anything to stop them. As soon as they caught sight of a black person, especially one walking alone, they pounced without being particular about his status. Pretending to recognize him as an escapee, they would lay hands on him and demand to see his papers. If he produced sufficiently impressive documents showing that he was free or was on an errand for some person of substance, they might decide to let him go. But if there was any weakness in his position—missing papers or a suspicious, frightened look—they would ignore all protestations and hustle him away. In most cases, the unfortunate person would soon be spirited southward and sold to a planter who gladly paid a good price without asking questions. Even children sometimes disappeared in this way.

Many property owners who considered themselves model citizens tolerated these abuses without complaint. Of slavery's many weird faces, one of the most revolting was that it made otherwise decent people numbly accept a prisonlike world, where even their own free lives were surrounded by the ugliness that wardens and guards see around them. Because they lived in fear of a slave uprising or a great wave of escapes, they welcomed anything that might terrify blacks enough to keep them in line. The terror these patrollers (or *patterolers*, as the word was commonly pronounced) created was acute enough to win a place in black folklore, with rhymes like:

> Run, nigger, run, patteroler'll ketch yer,
> Hit yer thirty-nine and swear he did'n tech yer.

When the Patapsco River valley had been little more than a backwater, its blacks had been safer from illicit slave-catchers than those in many other areas. But as its property values and population increased, the thugs had begun to move in.

One day, Molly had taken all her grandchildren and one or two neighbors' youngsters to a fair in the nearby port town of Elkridge Landing, which was some miles downriver from their home. At one point there was a commotion, and Molly spied four burly white men bearing down on her little group. She saw them quickly surround the children, stretching their arms wide to keep them from running.

Following their usual practice, they probably screamed, "Where are you from? Who do you belong to?" at the frightened children. The doughty little Molly later admitted that she was trembling, but she walked into the center of the group, pulled herself up grandly, and asserted something to the effect that these were "my slaves' children, of course." The thugs fell back awkwardly and touched their hats. To be a white woman with slaves was something that made sense to them, something worthy of respect.

The incident was over in seconds, and the younger children may hardly have realized that anything was amiss, beyond being puzzled by Molly's clever falsehood about "my slaves." Benjamin did understand, and it would prey on his mind during all the decades when he gave to many who knew him the impression of being serenely above the fray. It may have contributed to the tumultuous dreams, in full color, that troubled his nights throughout his life. This was not the last nor the worst of his encounters with horror, but it gave him his first understanding of what it meant to be black—and the power of simply being white—from which his quiet farm life had shielded him.

Although Benjamin Banneker was known as a free black all his life and clearly insisted on thinking of himself as free, he probably harbored a secret fear in a corner of his mind. The scrambled laws of that day may have technically jeopardized Molly's own freedom, for one ruling provided that a white woman who married a slave took on her husband's status. Molly insisted that she had given Banneka his freedom before she married him, but some feel that this arrangement might have been struck down if there had been a legal test, robbing the whole family of its freedom. Fortunately, nothing of the kind ever intruded, but the precariousness of his own liberty must have played a part in Benjamin's long tendency to avoid the spotlight.

Shortly after the terror incident had made him so aware of black–white issues, this mere child began thinking often about the plight of Native Americans. Already, at a very young age, he had caught on to a fact that most adults never grasped: that Indians could differ from each other as much as whites, blacks, or members of any other ethnic group. It was quite tragic that the Piscataway Indians of the Patapsco region, who wanted to be settled farmers and who went out of their way to befriend whites, were caught up in violence that was started by the burly and often warlike Susquehannock.

As far back as 1634, Father Andrew White, an early Jesuit missionary who had landed with the first Maryland settlers, wrote that the Piscataway showed "temperance and constancy in great affairs," adding that ". . . if they were once christian, they would doubtlesse be a vertuous and renowned nation." But the settlers were baffled by the twisted tribal politics and the occasional incidents of individual violence that made all the Native Americans seem menacing to them. A short-lived and complex alliance between the two tribes (trying to fend off the powerful Iroquois and Seneca) had confused the settlers and made them treat the friendliest Indians unfairly. The people of every colony still vividly remembered the past massacres of whites, especially the great Indian Massacre of 1622, which killed 350 whites—one-fourth of the Virginia colony's population. That had created a furor, even in England, leading King James I to end the private commercial venture known as The

Virginia Company and to make Virginia a Royal Colony. So now, although neighboring Maryland had no such local memories, the slightest sign of violence brought on the formation of defensive militias that massacred a great many Indians and sent more of them out of the area. There were even horrendous instances of Indians who had gratefully taken refuge with settlers in a time of chaotic disturbances being slaughtered by angry lynch mobs.

Most of this had happened years before Benjamin's birth, but when he heard the stories, he quickly formed his own impression that good and bad people alike had been wrongly treated, that potential friends had been made into foes. In doing this, Benjamin focused with his usual pinpoint accuracy on the key point that underlies all racism—the mistaken idea that the behavior of a few is a way to evaluate a whole group. Here, clearly, was a mind that would always have its own opinions, forming them with a judgment that matured early and then went on refining itself.

Just the reverse of his first terrifying experience came at about the same time in Benjamin's life, somewhere between eight and nine years of age. He met his first great friend outside the family, one who would influence his entire life, a Quaker schoolmaster who is thought to have been called Peter Heinrich. Although he depended on farming for a living, Heinrich had the intention of starting a school in the neighborhood.

Benjamin had gone on an errand for his mother one afternoon and was walking along a narrow dirt path toward his home when he encountered the young teacher. Heinrich was quite new to the area, having come as a volunteer because his church leaders thought this part of the Patapsco River region was growing fast enough to need education for young persons whose fathers were not rich enough to employ and house private instructors. The number of Quakers in Maryland had been climbing since

George Fox had come over from England in the late 1600s and had pinpointed Maryland as a state that would be receptive to Quaker ideas of equality and justice. Some Quakers had even moved to Maryland from their Pennsylvania base, for the latter state's religious freedom had a minimum requirement of belief in the Trinity, while Maryland had no limiting stipulations at all. It was also a state that had a number of "islands" of free black communities. The 1790 census showed about 8,000 free blacks in the state, but the number was probably only about 4,000 in the years of Benjamin's childhood.

The idea of a school was welcomed by the area's mayors. Once the subject was broached, in fact, these leaders realized that even more public schooling was going to be needed. Their eagerness to have him start a small school had enabled Peter Heinrich to insist on his own terms, which included the understanding that he had the sole right to decide whom he might admit to his school, with no restrictions. He had foreseen the possibility that any racial mixture in his classes might cause objections, and he had rebutted it in advance.

Something in Benjamin's eyes as they passed caught Heinrich's notice. It may have been a combination of the confident, steady look this young person had always had and the slight uncertainty about whites that had come over him since the incident with the patrollers. In any case, Heinrich saw something different from the downcast eyes that the children of slaves often thought it best to show when passing a white person. The schoolmaster spoke a gentle greeting and paused, introducing himself. He was startled at the eager way Benjamin responded on hearing that teaching was this man's business. Heinrich asked if the boy would like to come to his school, but Benjamin reluctantly said he didn't think he could take time away from the farm. The conversation was prolonged, with the Quaker finding it hard to tear himself away from this well-spoken lad whose accent sounded like that of an English person, yet with a different, foreign note. How could he have learned all these words, this fine language? Accounts tell us that Benjamin explained simply, "From reading the Bible."

Before they parted, it was agreed that at the very least Heinrich would lend Benjamin some books to expand his reading. At this point, there is a fork in the story: Over the years, most accounts related that Banneker never went to school a day in his life. But that assumption has been shifting a little in the course of continued research. It is now clear that one Joseph (or Jacob) Hall, another free black who said he lived in the same Elkridge area at that time (circa 1740), spoke of having been to the Quaker school rather briefly with Benjamin. "He was never fond of play or light amusement," one account quotes Hall as having said. "All he liked was to dive into books." Hall had no apparent motive for fabricating this story, except possibly the frequent tendency some people have to pretend to know a prominent person. His description of Banneker's studiousness sounds true. This supports the strong possibility that Benjamin did have a year or at most two in a classroom, but surely not more, because the need for help on the farm soon would have taken priority. In any event, it does not markedly change the widely believed fact that his formal education was exceedingly sparse, for it has long been acknowledged that he did have advice from a local teacher and that he was loaned a succession of important books over a period of several years. The essential fact that Benjamin was largely self-taught is unaffected. The most vital help was in the availability of great books, but there was very little time for actual tutoring, so he extracted and developed most of his knowledge on his own.

It is clear that Benjamin became familiar with many of the classics in this way, always astonishing the schoolmaster by returning them in a very short time and making a great many insightful remarks on the contents. From simple primers, he seems to have vaulted into volumes that were on the university level. Among the books were some from Heinrich's own library, far advanced beyond what he used in his schoolroom, including the works of Plato and Epictetus, histories of ancient Rome, and Newton's *Principia*, which Benjamin devoured in a few all-night readings, as if he had anticipated Newton's reasoning and was only skimming it to learn the proper words.

Heinrich realized he was dealing with a true genius. More than once, he told Benjamin that he hoped he could one day get him into the hands of a superior teacher, for he saw that the boy's mind was well above his own, frequently grasping points that Heinrich had not thought of. Before Peter was called away on another assignment, the two became more like friends than teacher and pupil, even though their ages were so far apart. This disregard for age differences would be a permanent trait in Banneker.

Through Heinrich's friendship and the exposure to so many fine books, Benjamin's speech began to be less biblical and closer to that of a well-educated gentleman. Some people can read the greatest works and remain unaffected in their own word choices. Most start to draw on their reading as a source of vocabulary enhancement. Only a few—Banneker among them—go on to develop a superior speaking and writing style.

Since Banneker remained a great favorite with his sisters and nephews all his life, he probably used family language when he was in that circle, just as many highly educated black persons say they consciously use "black talk" when they visit less culti-vated relatives or childhood friends. That practice, in fact, is no different from what happens in many other cultures. Italian Americans who speak elegant English may slip into a Sicilian or Neapolitan dialect when they talk with older relatives. Only persons who are not really confident of their own status fail to recognize that this is a courtesy to the elders and not a cause for embarrassment.

Incidentally, it was Peter Heinrich who proposed Benjamin's adoption of the spelling "Banneker" that has been known as his last name ever since. Oddly, the three generations of the family used three slightly different spellings: Banneka, Bannaky, and Banneker. Heinrich's choice of the third one apparently struck him as being more in the mainstream of the upscale Americans among whom he thought Benjamin was destined to belong.

～

Once he had formed the habit of devouring books, Benjamin continued to read voraciously all his life, to the full extent of what he could buy or borrow. And he balanced the reading experience with the less costly act of writing constantly. Once he adopted the habit of making entries in a daily diary, he held to it religiously, except for a mysterious period later in his life. However late it might be when his other duties were done, he would set about recording things he had learned from the day. These were mainly new observations and conclusions, including his nighttime study of the stars, rather than simply events. The loss of most of these diaries after his death was a tragedy, for the astronomical thoughts alone would doubtless have formed several volumes.

He often lay on the ground outside the cabin in those late hours, looking up into the million points of light that came through so dizzyingly at a time when there was no city brightness to dim them. He pictured other solar systems and other inhabited worlds, somehow conceiving of planets much like our own. And he imagined that those other people, returning his own stare, would see our sun as one more star and go on thinking themselves the center of all things. How he could have generated such concepts even before he acquired his own first rudimentary spyglass, we cannot imagine. But his own later writings make it clear that he did. To see mere specks of light and to reason—in the 1700s—that other intelligent beings might be looking back at our earth was a staggering exercise in pure thought. If the diaries had not been destroyed by arson, we would doubtless learn that he somehow found time to make hundreds of science-oriented entries even when his greatest years with finer instruments were decades away. This is documented by Banneker himself and some of his neighbors, who told of his untiring commitment to the regular diary entries. A small part of the contents has survived because Banneker later quoted some entries in the almanacs that he published in the idyllic last years of his life.

As he moved through his teens, it must have been frustrating for a mind that longed for time to read and learn and think to find that the farm duties pressing upon him multiplied. The death of grandfather Banneka had brought sadness and a realization of how much soul and thought the family lost, but it had not much changed the work routines, for Banneka had not taken real part in them for some years. Now, however, his father, Robert, was also growing frail at an early age, and that did alter the distribution of work. When he was little more than twelve, a full half of the farmwork fell on Benjamin's slender shoulders. There is no sign in anything he wrote to the end of his life that he resented this enough to consider rebelling. He saw the world, and his duty, for what it was. But he was human enough, as we know from a few incidents, to shed tears. And the deprivation of his precious thinking time may have created more inner rage than he ever showed, for later in life he did all he could to reduce and then almost eliminate the farmwork. This clash between physical labor and mental effort may, in fact, have been responsible for one curious period of apparent depression in his late twenties and thirties.

But a very real threat that he could not ignore began to weigh on Benjamin's mind long before he should have been burdened with adult responsibilities. This was the deteriorating condition of the soil on which his family and the whole Patapsco region depended. By planting tobacco year after year, they had been killing the land since before Benjamin was born. Nobody had a solution, for the whole region was geared to raising and exporting that one crop.

The entire river area, the basin, branches, and harbor site, had suffered mightily from the arrival of settlers since Captain John Smith first explored it in 1608. With its fish and other food sources, it had provided a balanced and healthy means of survival for the humans and animals of the region. But the decline in schools of herring and shad caused by dam construction, noticed in Benjamin's day, was to go on worsening decade after decade as waste was dumped.

The adjacent land areas naturally suffered from the sickening of the river. Tobacco planters with great tracts in the Patapsco region had begun to grow wealthy from world demand for their products even before the eighteenth century began. There were large landholders with names that would become nationally famous, and lesser settlers scattered all over the state. But the small town of Elkridge (originally called the Ridge of Elk and later Elk Ridge, named for a ridgeline that stretched to the west and south) became the acknowledged transport center around the turn of the eighteenth century because its location at a wide point on the river made shipments overseas easy and inexpensive. About this time, an anonymous British traveler wrote,

"This village does not deserve noticing on account of its size, as it contains only about 15 houses, 2 stores, and a few shops, but for being a place of business long before Baltimore was inhabited. Here all the business was conducted on a large scale, it being the deposit of all the tobacco raised for a considerable distance, where it was inspected and went to Europe."

By the time Banneker was born in 1731, most of the good land had been put to use for raising tobacco, and the surrounding area was thriving. The nearby town of Elkridge Landing had its own customshouse and inspection office, and the merchants who lived off this trade were building great homes.

The iron industry became second in importance to tobacco during Banneker's lifetime. Captain John Smith had first noticed red clay in the hills near the river, and the commercial exploitation of that started in 1755, when Caleb Dorsey established Elk Ridge Furnace. To encourage this added source of wealth, the General Assembly of Maryland ruled in 1719 that a person could acquire one hundred acres of uncultivated land along a river, but must start an operation within six months and complete it within four years. Dorsey's iron business would thrive into the nineteenth century, and the Ellicott family would add this to its holdings in 1820. But the furnace played no part in Banneker's thoughts and plans, as it was only for those who had major capital to invest.

Benjamin's grandfather, with the wisdom of his upbringing in an African area where farm mistakes could be critical, had told the family long since that planting the same crop over and over could be bad for the land. What he would not have learned in Africa is that tobacco is even harder on the land than most other crops. It leaches nutrients from the soil. Ideally, it should be planted for only two consecutive years, then the land rested for ten years. Clearly, a single small farmer could not live with such a schedule, nor could he turn away from the only product that could rely on established marketing facilities nearby. Banneker's family had no choice but to keep replanting tobacco while taking the greatest possible care of its own soil. The Banneker crop was always among the best in its neighborhood, but the specter of a general fall in quality was a worry that gnawed at the soul. Any talk of the future brought on silence, as everyone wondered whether there was to be a future at all. What would they do if there were no crop to sell? Or if they had a crop, but others didn't—and the whole area lost its links with the tobacco-buying world?

There were community meetings and talk of planting wheat, but it was always overridden by the majority. "How can we gamble our prosperity on a crop that we have never even tried in Maryland?" planters shouted at meetings when the issue was raised. "And even if it grows well, what are we to do with it, send it hundreds of miles to be made into flour? We'll all become poor. No, it's only tobacco for us!" Banneker only heard about those meetings. He had no part in them. But he could look at his own soil and see that the steady growing of tobacco was ravaging it. Only the wise ways passed down from old Banneka and the steadiness of his unusual son-in-law and grandson combined to keep the farm viable and the family afloat.

This life-and-death issue would prey on Banneker's mind for almost another half-century. We know that he kept writing letters to his sisters with instructions on care of the farm when he had to be away.

Yet his power of concentration was so great that none of this prevented him from thinking about the cosmos with the same wonder he had in childhood. "The soil I work with and the stars up there are all part of the same thing," he said. "They were both made for a purpose, and the purpose was good."

3

The Lurking Terror

Like many persons of his time, Benjamin never really had any youth. But while many other young colonists who were put to work before reaching their teens probably had at least an inner feeling of rebellion against parental rules and demands, that was not Banneker's way. He had a streak of maturity from infancy, an adult's understanding from age five. He made family problems his own before he was twelve.

Neighbors now thought of him simply as a fine, hardworking young man—not as noticeably a prodigy as when he was small. But he was, in fact, very unusual in the unique way that he managed the burden of work and suited it to his needs. Wasting no time or energy in fighting against the inevitability of work, Banneker nonetheless lived a life of contemplation for most of his waking hours. Because the nature of farmwork was mostly solitary, we know from diary entries that he could combine his physical labor with the deep thinking that was his greatest amusement. He kept at it as steadily as if he had an assignment, a timetable for how many unknowns would be explored each day or week. But because quality of thought was even more important than speed, he was forever reviewing things

around him with the innate precision of a scientist in his labo-
ratory. The soil he touched was a microcosm of the wider
world; he examined its makeup and texture. The acres around
him were part of the Patapsco River valley below and then of
the whole earth that dropped away beyond his horizon. The
planet itself was, in his mind, a sample that could lead to conclusions about the great sea of outer space. It takes someone
with a unique mentality to look down at the soil he stands on
and to picture what it would be like to set foot on the moon.
For an unschooled young person to have done that in a day
when only the most educated persons even knew there was a
solar system, the word *genius* is clearly applicable.

This dual absorption with abstruse thought and practical
labor may have caused Banneker to be less than normally interested in the opposite sex at that time. Or it could be that he had
a very low sex drive. In any case, he moved into his twenties
with little apparent interest in the young girls who looked admiringly when he passed them on an errand to the town below.
His dutiful concentration on the growing of tobacco seems to
have allowed no time for dalliance.

At twenty-two years old, he was a very confident young
man whose features and physique seemed to come mainly from
his father and grandfather. He had grown tall for that day—
probably 5'9" when the male average was 5'7"—straight as a
spear, and good looking, with regular features. His complexion
was rather dark. His own description—"I am of the deepest
dye"—may have been a slight exaggeration, for some observers
described him as only moderately dark, but it showed that he
was proud of his African background and not at all anxious to
minimize it. The unusual head of hair—the loose curls that
doubtless stemmed from his mixed heritage—was almost as
striking as it would be years later when people remarked on the
"mass of white ringlets." Benjamin's dominant feature, however,

was uniquely his own and not easily traceable to any known ancestor. It was a look of placid intelligence that seemed to belong to a person three times his age, more like an all-knowing old bishop than a bright young farmer. That look—more benign than yearning—must have been a deterrent to any young girls whose eyes had noticed his fine figure.

In 1753, the year he turned twenty-two, he was especially absorbed with the farm because there had been a beautiful summer and the family's tobacco crop had flourished well beyond the norm. It was not only plentiful, but of the very highest quality—a tribute to the wise legacy of his late grandfather and his ailing father, and also to Benjamin's prudent way of putting their farming wisdom to the maximum use. It was a very close-knit family and usually a harmonious one. His beautiful mother, Mary, made major contributions to their income by raising chickens, selling eggs and the many scents and spices that she had a special flair for concocting. Because there was only one general store, and that was in the town far below, the people who lived up on Oella's high ground were glad to learn of any new product she created. It took a whole day's journey to Joppa and back to buy more important equipment or supplies, such as a rake or a new plow. The same was true of the rare times when finer purchases were needed, such as shoes, brocades, glassware, or a book for Banneker. To limit such travel time, this clan—like most farmers in the area—had its own little workshop and mended implements, even shod its own two horses.

Because Robert was ailing, it was now grandmother Molly Welsh, the redoubtable Big Ma-Ma, who had quietly begun to take the lead again. Her daughter Mary had proved to be a capable and active woman and would be a great influence on Benjamin later in her life, but while her mother was alive, she very willingly let her have control. Without any words being said on the subject, it was Molly to whom Benjamin looked for decisions or for ultimate approval of whatever he decided on his own. And she had special plans for how this year's crop would be used to further expand their holdings.

A very exciting story about how that strategy played out gained currency when Shirley Graham, a black journalist and novelist, wrote a book about Banneker that has been called "a romanticized biography." She herself wrote that it was "constructed within the framework of little-known true facts," indicating that it was rounded out with considerable imagination. Because Graham was closely connected with civil rights activists through her marriage to W.E.B. Du Bois and was thought to have special insights about black history, this story gathered some adherents in Banneker's old neighborhood, and the details were further embellished. Significantly, the curator of the Banneker Memorial and some members of its governing board have been divided about using the Graham book for official purposes. What follows reflects accounts from all the known sources, eliminating what seems most improbable in order to come to what might have actually happened. The dialogue, based on what these sources have given, is obviously no more than an approximation of what might have transpired. Here and in another story we will come to further along, the use of unconfirmed accounts at least conveys the nature of events that Banneker faced, despite differences in detail. Fortunately, the great experiences he had later in life are supported by excellent documentation.

Here, the story is that Big Ma-Ma was looking forward to the tobacco proceeds to buy additional land. To maximize the gain, Banneker had proposed the adventurous idea of taking the crop to Baltimore for sale. His grandmother had protested that such a trip would be hazardous and had pointed out the obvious alternatives. A simple trip down the hillside to Elkridge Landing would have been the first thought. At this time, the town had no more than two hundred inhabitants and some twenty-five houses, but it did have one small finger pier that was used almost exclusively for tobacco exports, giving it significance in the tobacco trade. The next nearest possibility for selling the tobacco crop was the once-dominant port of Joppa. But its role as a marketplace was declining, and even its status as a county seat was endangered, which would have had a depressing effect on the number of bidders and the prices that were paid for commodities. By contrast, the aggressive surge of Baltimore, which would play a major role in Banneker's future, held the promise of premium prices. "Baltimore Town," as it was called when first incorporated in 1729, a scant two decades earlier, was thriving under the management of more aggressive merchants. Their daring had brought an aura of excitement and gathering prosperity. Just the year before, a brig from Baltimore had made a trip to Barbados, carrying tobacco, iron, flour, and other foods. This even prompted one Dr. John Stevenson to drop his medical practice and start sending shiploads of grain across the Atlantic. All the while, the city fathers had been very cleverly deploying the strategy of "non-importation" in concert with Annapolis and other major eastern cities. It was a form of resistance to the British policies, including the Stamp Tax, that infuriated the colonists. The Baltimoreans manipulated their role in ways that often seemed more self-serving than patriotic, but their tactics expanded trade and helped to aggrandize the city, making Benjamin's proposal hard to resist.

The low-key family debate went on for several days. Unusual as he was, Banneker could be as headstrong as any young man his age, and in the end, he had won Molly over to the idea of letting him make the daunting trip. Because the roads were too crude to permit use of a wagon, the precious tobacco, bundled in the form of "hogsheads," 32 inches in diameter, was pulled by packhorses, two of his own, two borrowed from neighbors.

On the morning of departure, the excitement was more like a sendoff to Europe rather than a trip of some twenty miles. Grandmother, father, and mother hovered apprehensively around the ever-confident Banneker. Three adoring sisters hopped around him and the horses, half wishing that girls could do such things, but shuddering at the risks their brother was so quietly about to undertake. And all were grateful that a senior person was joining him. This was an older family friend who was not really related to them, but who had always been called Uncle Ned. He was not quite as steadying an influence as they might have wanted, for he was given to sudden tempers and rashness. But they counted on Benjamin's firm hand to control this mercurial friend, while they somehow benefited from Uncle Ned's ten- or twelve-year age advantage.

Stories passed down about this three-day trip, however, tell of a disastrous beginning—owing precisely to Uncle Ned's carelessness. Just an hour after they set out, the pair was way-laid by a gang of "paterollers" out to corral slaves for resale at prices that had risen more than 100 percent since that day when Molly had routed a similar gang of thugs by pretending that the black children with her were her slaves. When five of these ruffians surrounded the two men and demanded to see their papers, Banneker quickly pulled out the documents proving that he was a free person. But he felt a terrible cold chill descend on him when he heard Uncle Ned mumbling excuses. The old friend had come away on this risky trip without re-membering to take the identification that no black could afford to be without.

Banneker spoke up, assuring the men that he had known Uncle Ned all his life, that he positively knew him to be a free man, that they could all turn and go back together to the home where Ned would show his papers. The self-styled enforcers would not be put off. Ned was a strapping male who would

The kidnapping of a free Negro. An unknown artist shows a free Negro of the era being subjected to the kidnapping that even a landowner like Banneker had to fear. (Library of Congress collection)

fetch a great price with no questions asked. Moving rapidly, because they realized that this smooth-talking younger black might come forward with arguments that would hamper their plan, they quickly threw a lassolike rope around their prisoner and hurried the screaming Ned away.

Horrified, Benjamin made a brief attempt to follow, but with the heavily laden packhorses lashed to his own mount, it was hopeless. He felt as if he were watching a murder committed. He knew his family would never see Uncle Ned again, because he would never submit to captivity. He would struggle and be beaten. He would fight back and be subdued by force. In the end, he would try to escape—in some erratic, poorly planned way—and die in the attempt.

All the confidence that Banneker possessed drained out of him. Lobbying for the trip to Baltimore had been a great

CAUTION!!

COLORED PEOPLE

OF BOSTON, ONE & ALL,

You are hereby respectfully CAUTIONED and advised, to avoid conversing with the

Watchmen and Police Officers of Boston,

For since the recent ORDER OF THE MAYOR & ALDERMEN, they are empowered to act as

KIDNAPPERS

AND

Slave Catchers,

And they have already been actually employed in KIDNAPPING, CATCHING, AND KEEPING SLAVES. Therefore, if you value your LIBERTY, and the *Welfare of the Fugitives* among you, *Shun* them in every possible manner, as so many *HOUNDS* on the track of the most unfortunate of your race.

Keep a Sharp Look Out for KIDNAPPERS, and have TOP EYE open.

APRIL 24, 1851.

Warning to Boston blacks. Conditions continued to worsen, so even midway into the nineteenth century and in a major city far to the north, blacks had to fear slave-catchers. (Library of Congress collection)

mistake. Why had he not checked carefully on Ned's preparations as well as his own? For the first time in his life, he had to admit to himself that he had blundered. Not even the hubris of youth could rid him of a raging wish to be dead. He slid off his horse, fell to the ground, and lay there panting and sobbing.

After a few minutes, he had an impulse to remount and turn rapidly for home, but he tried to think rationally about the right thing to do before acting. To go back and report the loss of Uncle Ned would do no good. A white person might go to the authorities, report the theft of a slave, and reasonably hope for a possible restoration, but for a black to make the report—in effect, to charge white persons with abduction—was un-thinkable. Even several decades later, when Benjamin Franklin founded a Society for the Rescue of Persons Held Illegally in Bondage, the number of such rescues was negligible. But in 1753, there was not even the pretense of a mechanism for re-porting these brutal events. Going home would have no effect except to calm Benjamin himself.

On the other hand, coming home a few days from now with the money Big Ma-Ma hoped for would at least be a mission accomplished. His every instinct argued against it. He wanted to go home more than anything in life. Mounting his horse and moving on toward Baltimore seemed unbearable. But his mind said it was the right choice. So he remounted and set out in the original direction.

⁓

Because of the interruption, it was late in the day before he arrived in Baltimore—too late to do any business. The rule, he knew, was for tobacco to undergo a quality inspection and be graded by British customs officials. These men had great power, for their decision actually determined the price as the tobacco was moved to a pier and sold for export to the mother country. Banneker pushed on to the harbor area, located the customs office, and tied up his horses near it in order to make the earli-est possible start the next morning. But he spent a most uncom-fortable night, trying to sleep a little on a pad of blankets that cushioned him against the hard paving stones, yet waking every few minutes for fear that his precious load of tobacco might be stolen in this world that had turned so harsh and unrelenting.

When the customshouse opened in the morning, Banneker soon learned that broad daylight could be more dangerous than darkness. A single British customs officer was on duty—a corrupt official who had to assess the goods before a buying agent made payment. The customs man was appalled to see so much fine tobacco being offered by a black, for it would surely infuriate the great planters who doubtless made payoffs to him for holding down the quantity of goods that would compete with their own. He must not let this black youth ruin his own reputation with the wealthy shippers. Sneering at Banneker, mocking his attempt to seem confident, he looked at the fine, lush tobacco leaves, beautifully cured, and asked, "Where did you get this? Probably stole it all, eh?"

The soft reply was "I raised it all, sir."

"Raised it where? Who do you belong to, anyway?"

"I belong to my own family. I'm a free person." Trembling, he showed his papers, holding them tightly with one hand.

The man looked briefly, paused hesitantly, but still insisted on protecting his own interests by getting rid of the threat. He reached across to the loads, fingered the leaves carelessly, making a disapproving face. "Well, I'd say less than a third of this is good tobacco. You'll get ten pounds for it, nothing more. The rest is not good enough to ship. It's confiscated."

Unaccustomed anger welled up in Benjamin, almost overwhelming the knowledge that he must not appear to quarrel with a white official. "Sir, I'm sure it's worth much more than that, even in Elkridge. I'd rather take it back there." He began to back his horses away.

"Not so fast there," the officer commanded. "You can't come in here trying to cheat the Crown, then pull out when you're caught at it." The man put a firm restraining hand on one of the packhorses.

"I have not tried to cheat, sir. I don't want to sell this here."

"Well, you won't sell it anywhere. It's confiscated."

Benjamin struggled to hold his tongue, but he glared with a steady look that startled the corrupt official. Luckily, a few other traders had begun to line up with their loads, and the officer saw that the conversation might be overheard. He tried to make a slight compromise that would still not enrage his wealthier patrons. "Look, you," he growled in a low voice. "I can confiscate this whole thing, because too much of it is bad goods. But I'll condemn only part of it and the agent will let you have fourteen pounds for the rest. Take that or take nothing!"

Even if this is more an account of Banneker's fears than an incident he actually suffered, it is highly significant, for he recorded many dreams that show how much he was haunted by the great danger surrounding all blacks. However factual the abduction of Uncle Ned may have been, such things were in every black person's mind every time he or she went out, fearfully clutching proof of identity. It was a subhuman condition, even for a free black. Here was a property owner whose life was that of a nonperson, almost unrecorded until he began a friendship with a white family years later. Even then, he had no mailing address of his own. When he went on to deal with white leaders, to question scholarly journals, and to be mentioned as a role model in the British Parliament, a letter to him would have had to be addressed through a white person. The account of his treatment at the hands of a customs official, therefore, is totally true to life and at least reflects what came to be the tone of his increasingly turbulent dreams.

Whatever Banneker actually suffered at the hands of the customs inspector in Baltimore, it was almost certainly a real robbery that was made all the more galling because he had to accept it wordlessly. To argue would have meant risking a total loss. In the end, he left with only that small fraction of what Big Ma-Ma had hoped to see him bring home. The money would allow them to get by until the next season, but there would be nothing to buy those extra acres they had dreamed about. All the youthful self-assurance that had made him so confident of turning a fine deal in this city had drained out of him, and his head slumped onto his chest as he watched workmen hastily setting flames to most of the beautiful tobacco he had labored so hard to produce. He moved slowly away with the empty packhorses, his face flooded with tears.

4

A Door Opens Wider

It is said that a stout Baltimore merchant named William Qualls had been standing near enough to witness young Banneker's misfortune in the Baltimore customshouse. Almost like a *deus ex machina*, Qualls came and spoke a few kind words to the shattered young man. As soon as he heard them, Benjamin recognized that this man was a Quaker, for he addressed him as "thee," and that was the language of Peter Heinrich, the Quaker schoolmaster who had first recognized the boy's genius and fed his mind with great books. William Qualls now talked soothingly to Benjamin, gradually quieting the horror within him. They spoke together about Peter Heinrich, and Benjamin felt as though the evil world of these last twenty-four hours was being pushed aside by the purifying recollection of how fair-minded some persons could be. Within a few minutes, Qualls had been struck, as people had been before, by Banneker's fine language and obvious high intelligence. He asked if Benjamin had time to come to his home and meet a friend who was staying with him. There could be only one answer to that.

Benjamin's horses were stabled by Qualls's groom just as attentively as if they belonged to a noble visitor. This was a world

Banneker knew and loved, not because the house was tasteful and he was well treated, but because here respect was a currency that had only one rate of exchange—its value never fluctuated.

The introduction that took place in Qualls's drawing room was to be one of the high points of Banneker's life. Qualls presented him to a small, dark-haired man who radiated alert intelligence. There was a mutual excitement in his meeting with Joseph Levi, a trader and investor who was extending his European interests to dealing with the New World. With the same talent Peter Heinrich had for understanding minds greater than his own, William Qualls had been prescient in bringing these two men together. For Levi, a man of the world who was at home in every capital of Europe, and Banneker, who had never been more than a few miles from his tobacco farm, shared a love for discovering and discussing abstract ideas. They were not satisfied with merely polishing what was already known. They loved things that were only half imagined or, better yet, ideas that seemed to be emerging for the first time.

The subjects they talked about that afternoon were not at all new to Joseph Levi. He had been passionate about the sciences for years, but it was the discovery of a young man like Banneker that engrossed him. He saw in Benjamin a mind that was leaping just as his own had once done to tame and embrace the unknown. No years or sophistication or command of many languages could blur the similarity between them in this one greatest trait. And as Levi's astonishment at Benjamin's intelligence increased, he introduced more and more subjects.

And so they talked of astronomy, gravitation, celestial navigation. One of William Qualls's servants brought them beverages, which they sipped unthinkingly, with no pause in the conversation. Benjamin was almost panting for breath as he sprinted to catch as many facts as possible. He was using Levi's words as a climber uses footholds and handholds, pulling himself up to new conclusions, new uses for each principle, new ways to invert an equation. When Levi brought up calculus, he was amazed to realize that Benjamin had learned and nearly mastered it—on his own—almost as if he had independently reinvented Isaac Newton's mathematical discovery.

At one point, Levi took a watch from his pocket to check the hour, for he knew that others would soon be waiting for him. Benjamin stared at the bright face of the watch and heard the tick it was producing. He had heard of clocks but never seen one. Now he was seeing his first watch, and he knew at once that this was something he had waited for all his life.

The very word "time" had been magical to Benjamin from early childhood, and this fascination had intensified over the years. A sundial he had made stood in the yard outside his cabin. His musings on time seem to have prefigured some of the intuitions of Planck, Einstein, and Bohr by more than a century and a half. Was time there if no one was observing it? he had wondered. Did it change when observed? Did it change if someone was running fast? Was it related to light? Levi had been startled when he spoke of the ratios between the watch's wheels and found that Benjamin knew about diameters, degrees, minutes, seconds, meridians. But when the young man's questions ranged to the texture of time, whether it had substance and weight, Levi knew that here was an investigative power he had scarcely seen before.

On that day in 1753, Benjamin's excitement made him feel faint when Joseph Levi, reluctantly moving to leave, said he wanted Benjamin to keep the watch, wind it every day to make it run, and think about how it related to the positions of the whole solar system and the stars beyond it. Benjamin protested that he could not keep anything so valuable. "Hold it while I am away," Levi said. "Then we can decide what to do with it when I return."

Levi never came back. He was killed in a shipwreck on his next voyage. When Benjamin heard about it months later, it was the greatest sadness he had ever experienced. He felt sure—wrongly—that he could never know a greater unhappiness. Indeed, although he would have another great and long friendship, there would never again be an encounter like the two hours he and Levi had spent together.

He went home with two terrible pieces of news to tell his family. Yet his mind was absorbed with all the new worlds that he was determined to explore. The happiness of such adventure somehow made loss and disappointment shrink, just as perspective makes parts of a picture grow smaller. His analytical mind even studied this reaction, studied itself, considering the guilt it should be feeling for experiencing happiness while poor Uncle Ned was a captive. But he was orderly about putting each part of the equation in its place, refusing to beat himself over what could not be helped.

~

Long after the report to his family had been made and wept over, what dominated Benjamin's thoughts was the watch he was guarding, wrapped in a clean towel and hidden under a floorboard in his cabin. He longed to take it apart so he could see exactly why it ticked and moved with such precision. Joseph Levi had only told him to keep it and wind it, not to risk destroying it. What if opening the case made it fly into bits that could never be put back? He was supremely confident of his ability to analyze anything he could see, but he wondered if there was not a chance that this little mechanism contained pieces too small for unaided eyesight to see properly. Or that the almost lifelike nature of this invention would never recover from being opened and exposed.

Days passed—he never said how many—with the watch being taken out, wound, and considered from every angle. He must have known from the start that he would finally open the precious object, but there was a point to this long delay. With each new reexamination, he knew a little more of what to expect, or thought he did. So when, late one night, he finally put a large white cloth over his worktable and began to pry open the back cover, he was not as nervous as he had expected to be. Twenty minutes later, he was becoming much more distressed. Nothing was flying apart, but the wonderful consistency of the escapement was craftmanship of such fineness that his hope of learning to reproduce such a thing had disappeared. He saw at once that someone had used tiny tools made just for this purpose and undoubtedly had magnification to facilitate every move. Humbly and with a sense of defeat, he thought how foolish he had been—a poor farmer whose best possessions were primitive had somehow thought he could reproduce a man-made jewel that must surely be worth more than his entire farm earnings amounted to in five years. He was only gladdened and grateful for the fact that no one, especially Joseph Levi, knew what foolish thoughts he had harbored.

The fit of depression didn't last long. It wasn't a jewel-like watch he had particularly wanted to make, he reminded himself. Rather, it was the concept he longed to understand. Just how did this collection of little wheels reproduce the timekeeping properties of a sundial? That was it! Time was the elusive element without which there would be no universe. It was the moment-to-moment movement called time that seemed to keep all of creation's atoms in alignment. Without time's constant sequencing, time's meticulous way of arranging things in order, everything that is or appears to be would be a collection of frozen atoms, of random inert objects and corpses. Now, he reasoned, if one understood why this watch's action could be so precisely in lockstep with time, might one not begin to know the nature of time itself?

True, the ability to make a watch would have brought him closer to such understanding, he thought. But did it really have to be a small watch, with parts so tiny that the whole process was made far more difficult? Suppose he could capture the essence of this timekeeping principle in a larger and more manageable form . . .

And so the idea for what would become Banneker's wooden clock was born. After drawing a careful design of how the watch's parts fitted together, then taking it completely apart and studying the mathematical ratios of the gearwheels to each other, he had his strategy for making a large clock whose seconds, minutes, and hours exactly paralleled those of the watch. It would all be made from wood, the one material to which he had easy access and that he could fabricate without the problems caused by miniaturization. Banneker never knew that another wooden clock had been made in 1713. John Harrison, the great British watchmaker who eventually revolutionized seamanship by devising a timepiece accurate enough to help sailors in finding their longitude, made one of his first clocks chiefly of wood. In the splendid book *Longitude*, published in 1995, Dava Sobel wrote about her subject's early pendulum clock: "Aside from the fact that the great John Harrison built it, the clock claims uniqueness for another singular feature: It is constructed almost entirely of wood." She did not know that Banneker ended that "uniqueness" only four decades later. Harrison's selection of material was made in order to avoid rust and the need for lubrication. Banneker's choice was dictated by sheer necessity; wood was all he had.

The work went on for several months. During that time, no one was allowed in his cabin—any cleaning was done by Banneker himself. He gave only minimal attention to the farm, and his father was not too understanding of the project. But when it was finished and moving and regularly striking each hour, all the neighbors came to marvel. The old feeling that he was a super-human prodigy—which had flourished when he was a small boy, but then ebbed as he appeared to be no more than an estimable young man—took hold in everyone's mind again. Banneker would always remember with pleasure that his father had lived to see this moment. Practical-minded as Robert Bannaky was, it was not lost on him that half the people of the Patapsco area seemed to know what his son had made, and scores of those wanted to come into his cabin and see with their own eyes the great wooden clock that ran and ran and ran, the clock that was always exactly right in telling how much of the day had gone by, when the sun would dip, and when all the light would be gone.

Everyone marveled except Banneker. He was pleased to have proved to himself that his understanding of the gear ratios was correct. He was glad to have reassembled Joseph Levi's watch to perfection, and he went on dreaming, even after hope had really died, that his friend would somehow show up to reclaim it. It was good to feel, too, that he could take up watch-making as a trade with very little more study. That, however, was not what he wanted. Understanding the clock was supposed to bring him a greater grasp of time itself, but it had not. Creating a clock had taught him a little more about the math involved and a lot more about woodworking. But now what? The concept of time would continue to be a subject for future study and meditation. Joseph Levi would have been quick to believe if some intuition had told him that later in life, this Banneker would be writing profound thoughts about time, writing these deep ideas with a simple clarity that made great concepts easily understandable to thousands of people.

The fact that his wooden clock became part of Banneker's legend, always prominently mentioned in any description of the man, is actually an indication of the tendency to underrate him by focusing on his lesser skills, as if his color made them more surprising. Discovering the principle of the watch and then translating that to a large wooden mechanism was brilliant because he had done it alone, but it was not new. Making the clock itself represented analytical ability, persistence, and craftsmanship—but not genius. It demeans the memory of a true intellectual to think a piece of clockwork was his pinnacle. What counts most is Banneker's investigation of time itself in a day when few colonists even kept track of time on an hourly basis. Important hours of the day were usually marked by church bells or occasionally by the blast of a town cannon. Yet here was a farmer who, even when he studied the raising of tobacco, related every step of the process to time. In Philadelphia, David Rittenhouse had made numerous elegant timepieces for wealthy families, and several other Americans had made clocks, but none of them is known to have thought about the *nature* of time. That was where Banneker stood alone.

～

The account of Qualls and Levi is another part of Banneker's early life that is only half seen through the mists of time, but in this case there is much stronger confirmation that an event of this magnitude occurred.

For one thing, the intervention of a Quaker like William Qualls has a certain credibility when seen against the tapestry of Banneker's life. If it is true, as Samuel Hopkins has pointed out, that Benjamin Banneker's career was part of the early colonial trend leading toward the American Revolution of 1776 and all our subsequent ideas of human rights, there should be greater recognition of the Quaker contribution to the whole saga. Banneker knew that one of the most tireless and effective abolitionists was a Quaker preacher named Anthony Benezet, who wrote books opposing slavery, traveled throughout the colonies speaking out for his cause, and never abated in the face of harsh opposition and physical threats. His success in operating a night school for blacks led him to make a simple statement that was considered startling in that day: "With truth and sincerity, I declare that I have found among them as great a diversity of talents as among an equal number of whites." It has already been noted that the first Quakers came to Maryland because they felt that this colony's rules and rulers were most consonant with their own idea of justice for all. Then their presence and influence in the state kept working to turn high principles into practical reality. And although there may have been other occasions, we know of at least three times when a Quaker appears to have behaved toward Benjamin Banneker in a way that made a major difference in his life.

Significantly, the three-and-a-half-century history of the Quaker movement has been replete with examples of followers who acquired wealth while minimizing the importance of money. George Fox, the sect's founder, told his people in 1652 to "beware the deceitfulness of riches." They followed his lessons, yet somehow were spectacular successes in business. In England, they founded such great institutions as Barclays and Lloyd's, and they were behind the rise of iron production that accompanied the Industrial Revolution. Despite being a small sect and suffering persecution after the restoration of King Charles II, they ranked high among the eighteenth-century families with more than 100,000 pounds in wealth. Not only because they had helped him, but also because their ways made so much sense to him, Banneker was naturally attracted to the Quakers. He was drawn to their example of how it was possible to prosper while holding fast to their discipline, their principles of nonviolence and absolute honesty. He was attracted to the fact that Friends lived frugally, gave each other loans and mutual

OBSERVATIONS

On the Inslaving, importing and purchasing of

Negroes;

With some Advice thereon, extracted from the Epistle of the Yearly-Meeting of the People called QUAKERS, held at *London* in the Year 1758.

Anthony Benezet

When ye spread forth your Hands, I will hide mine Eyes from you, yea when ye make many Prayers I will not hear; your Hands are full of Blood. Wash ye, make you clean, put away the Evil of your Doings from before mine Eyes Isai. 1, 15.

Is not this the Feast that I have chosen, to loose the Bands of Wickedness, to undo the heavy Burden, to let the Oppressed go free, and that ye break every Toke, Chap. 58, 7.

Second Edition.

GERMANTOWN:
Printed by CHRISTOPHER SOWER. 1760.

Quaker opposition to slavery. Title page of a 1760 book by renowned Quaker writer and preacher Anthony Benezet, titled *Observations on the Inslaving, Importing and Purchasing of Negroes.* (Rare Book Division, Library of Congress) help as a matter of course. However, there was a streak of independence in Banneker that made him slow to join this sect. But the likelihood—not firmly established—that he eventually chose the Quaker faith lends a touch of confirmation to the idea that a Baltimore gentleman like Qualls may well have added his name to that of Peter Heinrich among Benjamin's happiest memories.

Whether there was really a Joseph Levi or not is another question that calls for deduction rather than assertion. Though there is no recorded evidence of the name, it is certain that a new outside influence made a major difference in Banneker's life at that stage. Two things are fact beyond doubt: the existence of a watch on which he based his celebrated wooden clock and the inspiration to push ahead with an even greater passion for astronomy and thoughts about the cosmos. Two decades later, another great friendship would provide finer telescopes and other instruments, but those only facilitated the studies and thoughts that began to consume Banneker in his twenty-second year—at about the time of that Baltimore trip.

That he made a wooden clock in 1753 has never been in any doubt. It was seen and remarked on by numerous reliable persons. More than forty years after Banneker made it, a visitor to his cabin spoke of seeing it—with all its systems operating perfectly. This was Susanna Mason, of Harford County, who wrote of being in his home when the clock was forty-three years old and still running well. Although that is the only account at such a late date, there is absolute verification from many sources that the clock was running well in 1773, twenty years after it was made. There had to be an original watch from which Banneker learned the inner workings of his clock. And a watch, in that day, would have been far too costly an item for this young man to purchase. That means it was surely given or loaned to him by someone sufficiently impressed to hand him a thing of great value. (A loan that he returned is likelier, for it is known that Banneker purchased a watch for himself toward the end of his life. He would not have gone to such an expense if, as the story goes, Levi's watch remained as a permanent possession.) But whether or not the donor's or lender's name and description are exact, there was almost certainly a meeting and discussion of this kind, and it was a milestone in the life of Benjamin Banneker.

Much more than the timepiece, it was the excitement over astronomy that made such a difference. It would seem that the fateful talk stirred Banneker to find money for a small telescope, for he began to look more seriously at the stars night after night. The magnification could not have been at all satisfactory, probably not very much better than the naked eye. But the focusing effect helped to identify different objects, and the attempt to see became a habit. When the temperature permitted, he would lie on his back outdoors and often stay there until the first light of dawn began to wash away the starlight (possibly contributing to the premature rheumatism that would plague him later). At other times, he would look from a cabin window. Either way, he was recalling Levi's or somebody else's account of the constellations, meticulously collecting and assembling data that he would later refine to become a superb astronomer. And above all, when he looked at a star, he was conscious of literally seeing the past, because the light that reached his eyes was a picture of what had been there many years before. He had begun to think about time and the cosmos in a way that would not become part of humanity's general consciousness until the twentieth century.

5

The Great Unknown

Something mysterious and terrible happened to Banneker in 1759.

Several years of contentment had followed the making of the clock and the heightened interest in science. Benjamin had applied himself equally to thinking about time, pondering the cosmos, and the more practical issue of raising tobacco. Applying his conceptual power, he analyzed the whole process of farming and broke it into thirty-six distinct steps. There is no record of what purpose this was supposed to serve or whether it made a difference in the next season's crop. Nor is it known whether his father found it a source of pride or a somewhat excessive application of his brilliant son's scientific ways. In any case, Banneker's analytical farming methods produced crops that were the envy of the neighborhood.

But when Banneker was twenty-eight years old, he somehow lost the intellectual energy that had been a vital part of him, and this void lasted for well over a dozen years. Some historians believe there was a romantic episode with a tragic ending that virtually destroyed him. Whatever the cause, it is certain that something life-altering happened to Banneker in 1759, something of a kind that had never before disturbed the even tenor of his existence. Outwardly, life on the family's farm was unchanged. They planted tobacco, orchard crops, and vegetables with good success. They had beehives and a variety of livestock. By supplying their own meats and vegetables, they were largely self-sufficient. Banneker himself had become the owner and manager of the entire property the year before. His father, Robert, had died prematurely but not unexpectedly in 1758, another victim of the abuses he had suffered in his early slave days and the difficulty many Africans had in adapting to Maryland's winters. Although the death of a parent can sometimes be a reminder of one's own mortality, the loss of his father was not a jolt, as it had been expected for several years. Nor was the burden of work enough greater to have brought on the mysterious collapse of his mental vitality.

He went on working to keep the farm operating, for nothing would make him abandon the other family members who depended on him, but he became a hollow shell. All his interest in science, in the world around him, in the cosmic subjects that had always dominated his thoughts, evaporated. Even the disciplined habit of keeping his journal was abandoned for more than twelve years.

The only evidence of anything other than farmwork are a few stories about purported dreams he had. He wrote these as if he were recording his own dream experiences, but they are long and detailed accounts that read more like fictitious morality tales. They may have been written in the hope of being published, but this was long before he had any idea of how to go about writing for profit or of taking up any form of livelihood other than farming, and nothing came of them. There may have been more of these than the three known ones, but if so, they probably perished along with so many of his belongings in the fire after his death.

One such dream story that did survive, a very long one, was written in October 1762, a typical product of this period of apparent distraction. Although there is no evidence that Dante's *Inferno* was among the books loaned to him by Peter Heinrich, the idea of a visit to the netherworld by a living person makes that seem a possible source. This early story differs in mood from the distresses of the real dreams in his last years. It is also interesting as evidence of the considerable growth of Banneker's writing skill between this 1762 date and his 1790s efforts. By the latter date, regardless of color, education, or working background, he would show himself to be one of America's fine writers, with a complete mastery of every detail and a flawless style. But here, in an excerpt from the dream story he wrote at age thirty-one, although he shows high imagination, a large vocabulary, and great descriptive ability, there are still occasional grammatical errors and awkward phrases:

> I thought I was dead and Beheld my Body lay like a corps, there seemed to be a person in the appearance of a Man his Raiment somewhat of a sheep skin or bright fawn colour, who said follow me. He ascended a Hill on the Top of which was a Large Building. The outside appeared strongly built, of large rough stone. I followed my guide into the House, but did not at first see the beauty of it to the full. It seemed white and bright, and a Large Company sitting, such a number as I never beheld. The farther we went in, the Brighter it appeared, and more like the reflection of the Sun . . . There appeared a sweetness & composure in every countenance, far beyond what I ever seen in any person while in the Body . . . I looked to see if I could Distinguish Men from Women but could not . . . I looked to see from whence the Light came, but could not discern either window or opening. I then asked my guide what is this place. He answered Heaven. Then I looked to see what they sat on, but could not discern

either seats or form. The more I looked, the more I admired and wanted to sit with 'em, but could not tell how. My guide turned about to go out and look'd at me and said follow, but I was so much delighted that I was unwilling to follow . . .

Then the guide turned on the left hand . . . until we were at a lofty grand arch of great width where we entered a Large Room . . . which appeared grandly wainscoted and beautifully painted with different colours. The first sight of this beautiful room abated my sorrow, which was very great, while we came down the descent, from leaving the other. I had but just time to take a view of this fine place before a number of persons richly dressed passed us who smelled so strong of Brimstone, that I seemed allmost suffocated. All of them were talking to themselves, and before they came to us they looked well, but when they came near, there appeared a blackness on their lips and seemed to mutter to themselves . . . I was seized with horror and asked my guide what is this place and what are these. He answered this place is Hell and them are Miserable forever . . . as I looked round there appeared in my view a Woman Friend, plainly dressed in a green apron, whom I remembered well when I was young. I often took notice of her for the Solidity of her Deportment, particularly in Meeting. I eagerly made up to her and said what art thou among the Miserable, tell me, tell me what brought thee hither. She wept and said, no wrong that I have done between Man & Man, but unfaithfulness and disobedience to my God brought me hither . . . We met many like the other, in appearance and smell, that I seemed allmost suffocated with Brimstone, I then in great bitterness of spirit said to my guide, tell me am I to remain here forever. I thought a little time past if I had died I had secured an Inheritance among the first we saw. My guide stood and looking steadfastly at me said thou art not to remain here, but to return to the World again. If thou art faithful to thy God, thou mayest have an inheritance among the first, but I have something else to show thee. He went a little farther, when another arch appeared . . . wherein abundance of people were assembled, to worship and saying Amen, Lord have mercy upon us, Christ have mercy upon us, these appeared more plane in their dress and looked whiter. I said to my guide these are not Miserable too, and he said these are Miserable, these are they who thought to be saved by a profession of Religion, but have not the white robes of Righteousness . . . I thought I knew many of these who allso looked at me, as if they knew me . . . I again entreated my guide to let me go, he walked gently out of this place and came again into the entrance of this House which is wide with a Large Gate, here stood a number in Black or dark Clothes . . . I saw an Intimate Friend whom I much loved (this friend died in About a Month after) coming towards the Gate and two persons conducting him he looked very Sorrowful on me, and I on him. I asked him art thou going amongst the Miserable, what is thy offence, what has thou done, Tell me. He answered beware of Covetousness, and the love of Money, that brought me hither, we both wept much and were greatly troubled . . . my guide had me to a place, where there was just room to go Out, he stood and look'd at me, and earnestly said thou are now going into the World again. Remember what thou hast seen, it is not enough to be honest to Man, thou must be honest and faithful to thy God . . . then I awoke, but the horror and distress I felt on my mind I am not capable of Expressing. I seem as if I fetched my breath in a room where Sulfur & Brimstone were burning. . . Thought I could not live many Hours if the Almighty in the Extendings of his Boundless Goodness had not Reguard to me a poor unworthy Creature and caused that Suffocating smell to pass from me . . . and enabled me to vent my sorrow in many Tears, after which my toss'd mind was favoured with a Calm.

Assuming that this is an invented story, not a true dream, some of the things he writes of having seen can be considered indicators of principles that he believed humans should live by. The fact that in Heaven he "could not distinguish men from women," for example, appears to show how wrongly we exaggerate the distinction between the sexes. Also, the composure and the lack of seats seem to describe a world where neither tension nor gravity exist, making for perfect mental and physical comfort without having to seek repose. The second room, seeming as beautiful as the first, may well demonstrate that appearance is not everything and that one fine line separates Heaven from Hell, largely created by the dead themselves if they know they have disobeyed their God. And the third room, full of people who are mouthing religious words and phrases, shows that they failed to realize what God really wanted from them, and that their former confidence about being saved by displays of religiosity does them no good in eternity. This last thought might even be related to Banneker's long reluctance to join any of the established faiths that held some appeal for him, perhaps questioning the sincerity of the fellow parishioners he would be associated with.

Were it not for these dream stories, there would be no sign whatever that Banneker did any significant thinking or writing between 1759 and the early 1770s. It was as if the great mind that had always been captivated by the beautiful logic of all creation now rebelled against a world that had become ugly or irrational. Even though the dream is recounted with vivid imagery, the religious points it makes are somber, octaves lower in tone than the soaring views of creation that either the young Banneker or the Banneker-to-come could conjure up.

What could have caused this aggressive thinker to shift into low gear? True, there was the ongoing worry about the condition of the land. There were occasional poor crop years, but nothing of that sort seemed capable of turning such a balanced mind away from its intellectual interests. So the limited coterie of "Banneker watchers" turned to another of the unconfirmed accounts that writer Shirley Graham considered "convincingly probable." It was the tale—or perhaps more accurately, the theory—of a chillingly tragic romance.

In 1759, the story goes, Banneker was attracted to a slim, vivacious young woman whom he encountered in a marketplace near Elkridge Landing. She is said to have been rather exotic in appearance, possibly from one of the Caribbean islands. Although she was a slave, she had an unusually independent manner and quickly agreed to see Benjamin again. He suggested times when they might meet, and just a few brief conversations were enough to stir his quiet spirit to strong emotion. For the first time in his life, he understood why the subject of love had such a powerful effect on so many people. He was deeply in love and certain that this was to be a lasting attachment. Her name, Anola, kept singing in his mind without letting up. She returned his affection and was delighted with his plan to buy her from her master, set her free, and then make her his wife.

Banneker went to see the master and was staggered by the man's rudeness and furious response to his proposal. It was the first of several attempts. Banneker even called on his Baltimore Quaker friend, William Qualls, to intervene. He increased the amount of his offering price to a sum that was far beyond the norm. But the owner's anger only mounted. He seemed outraged that this black had the arrogance to negotiate with him, and the fact that he was a *free* black made no impression at all. There was no such thing, as he saw it: All blacks should be slaves, and none should be allowed to come and bargain with a white man. (One version of this story includes the overheated twist that Banneker offered to become the man's slave himself if he would promise to let him marry Anola and never part them. Predictably, this roused the master to new heights of fury. Even allowing for the irrational behavior that love can produce, it is unthinkable that Banneker would have wounded his own family in that way.)

Each time he left with a negative answer, Banneker became more worried that Anola would somehow suffer for having helped to create this deeply resented situation. And he was right, for the master took revenge by shooting Anola dead, and as one account tells it, he ended by turning the gun on himself. However, there is no public record of any such happening. All the versions of what happened would seem to indicate that the master was sexually obsessed with the girl and was enraged to learn that she preferred a black man. In that case, poor Banneker would have been desolate, not only over his own loss, but over the guilty feeling that he had brought about Anola's death. For that reason the story has had a certain appeal because it would appear to give a possible cause for the despondency that created the long void in his life.

But the search for a reasonable theory for this fallow period in his life could turn, with greater probability, to the chance that Banneker was homosexual. His gentle manner, which was mentioned repeatedly by Martha Tyson and by other acquaintances, although a totally unscientific indicator of sexual orientation, might make some more inclined to believe this. If such were the case, he would have known the truth about himself long before his twenty-eighth year, but considering the inconsistency of human emotions, it is possible that the constraints of the era would have made him put off facing the fact. He would not have been able to simply "come out of the closet" and go on with his life. In his day, such an admission would have made him a pariah or a convict. It is easy to imagine a person in such a dilemma delaying a resolution, working doggedly at his farm and his scientific thoughts. Then, at age twenty-eight, an inner urge might have compelled him to confront the issue, perhaps attempting a homosexual relationship and being disastrously rebuffed. Consequently, he might have been left to face a long lifetime of solitude ahead, suddenly seeing the world as an ocean of loneliness, making all his other interests seem insipid and hard to bear.

Considering the nature of his solitary life and the lack of firm evidence that any woman ever entered it, this alternate view appears somewhat likelier than the story of a heterosexual romance. But, although plausible, there is no historical evidence to support it.

Under the circumstances, a third possibility is more viable. Instead of the sex-based causes, suppose that here, instead, was a person with a low sex drive, regardless of orientation. In his case, the powerful urges are cerebral ones, pure thought and a hunger to know more and more. The simple, rather primitive sources at hand to feed this quest may have seemed sufficient for a while, but then his eager mind found itself facing a blank wall. After coming to suspect that those specks of light in the sky hid whole other worlds, he would have had no way of seeing more with a tiny telescope and no hope of ever buying the costly equipment that whites of a certain class used in their studies. His mind would have been like that of a bright child who is locked in a closet for years and goes nearly mad with the need to know more—or who vegetates, knowing the crack of light under the door will never allow him to see more. Less dramatically, Banneker may have simply tired of making notes about thoughts that he had no way to substantiate. His intellect, finding nothing more that it could profitably explore, was facing a void. He might have been like one of the examples in Thomas Gray's "Elegy Written in a Country Churchyard," a poor peasant whose innate capacity for great good or great evil is smothered by his meager circumstances. If this part of his history must be deduced without absolute proof, this seems a likelier—and in some ways more intriguing—explanation than any Freudian scenario. And it makes it easier to understand why the coming of the Ellicott family to the Patapsco region would bring a new dawn for Benjamin Banneker.

6

⁓

Enter the Ellicotts

T he agricultural and commercial awakening that the Ellicotts created in the Patapsco area affected the whole of Maryland and eventually the nation. In the course of that, they were able to rouse the dormant intelligence of what may have been the finest mind in the region. Their arrival and the technologies they introduced brought an end to Banneker's twelve-year mental hibernation and revived his old curiosity about science and the world around him.

This remarkable Quaker family never owned a single slave, proving the falseness of the notion that farming could not prosper without slave labor. Although most of their success was achieved in industry, they did also have extensive farm operations, using free, wage-earning workers, that were profitable. Having originated in Devonshire, England, the first Andrew Ellicott had prospered as a wool maker for a time, but was hit by financial reverses that made him look to the colonies in North America. He selected Bucks County, Pennsylvania, as the place for a new start.

Because the family reused the same few given names, confusing most accounts of the Ellicotts who eventually came to

Maryland, it is important to keep the generations straight. The son of this first Andrew was named Andrew II. He married a local Pennsylvania girl, and had five sons—Joseph, Andrew III, Nathaniel, Thomas, and John. They were in such poor circumstances for a time that they had to work as laborers and some of their children had to live with other relatives. But in 1766, eldest son Joseph came into an inheritance, a very large property in Cork, Ireland. He went back only long enough to sell the estate and returned to America as a wealthy man. At that point, the brothers conferred on how to make the most satisfying use of the fortune. They found both religious and commercial reasons to move to Maryland, which they thought to be more progressive and fairer in its insistence on human equality.

The next big decision was to make the relatively sparsely populated Patapsco region their base. They investigated the region with numerous trips and surveys in 1771 and 1772. They bought land called "The Hollow," cheaply priced, yet within ten miles of the very promising port of Baltimore. All of them were inventive, adventurous, and willing to put their shoulders into the physical work of developing their holdings. They even did their share of manual labor in extensive road-building that made their lands more accessible. These Ellicotts were serious people who could stay the course, and it gradually became known that they had actually purchased much more land than anyone realized. It was a two-mile stretch of river-front property upriver, and two of the brothers had hacked their way through dense brush to survey and prepare for a road connecting their lands with Elkridge. There is no surer way of raising the value of isolated land than by opening a transport link to a busy population center.

A series of coincidences, ranging from slight to amazing, linked the Ellicotts to Banneker. Devonshire, where they originated, happened to be in the part of England where Molly Welsh had been born. The eldest brother and leader, Joseph Ellicott, was an inventive man who made clocks as a hobby, and one of his clocks came to involve Banneker. In an even more significant way, brother Andrew III (also known as Major Ellicott after his service in the Revolutionary War) was to impact Banneker's life in 1791, some two decades after coming to the Patapsco, when he became the surveyor of the nation's capital.

The happiest coincidence of all was that Andrew Ellicott and his brothers had a young nephew, George, who was a prodigious amateur scientist and astronomer. George's daughter later said he was such an enthusiast that he would lecture on astronomy to anyone in the neighborhood who was willing to listen. This same young George was to become Banneker's great friend and collaborator in years of scientific thought and experimentation.

~❧

The relationship with the Ellicott family began in the early 1770s, when Banneker heard that interesting new buildings were being erected and fascinating new machinery installed down by the river. It was as if an alarm clock had sounded in his brain. He went to take a first look, was soon intrigued enough to make notes on what he had seen, and then began taking time for the long trip down to the riverfront every few days.

It seemed that an old hope of Banneker's finally had a chance of being realized. He discovered that a family with enough capital and energy to make a great change was urging the farmers of the area to begin what had long been discussed—to shift to wheat as a principal crop. But now it was more than mere words or angry meetings. At huge financial risk, the Ellicotts were making this an attractive alternative. In a remarkably short time, they were constructing a mill and having success in convincing the people of the area that they could create a much better future by raising wheat instead of tobacco and selling it to the Ellicotts for making flour.

Banneker did not immediately make the switch from tobacco to wheat on his own farm, for he was always very conservative about tinkering with the fundamentals of his livelihood, but he began making visits to the new flour mill the Ellicotts were about to open. His inventive mind was being roused by the sight of special devices they had created to make their mill more efficient. It was, in fact, a harbinger of the Industrial Revolution, a foretaste of automation. He was often seen inspecting the gears and sprockets of the mill machinery with as much fascination as he had once looked at the first watch he ever saw. He admired the simple "hopper boy," a large rake-like machine that could push ground meal from the loft to a chute without the presence of a workman. And he quickly saw that the "elevator"—a belt with scoops—could move grain in a variety of ways that had previously required many men.

On these visits, Banneker also began to patronize the Ellicott Company's store, where there were refreshments and convivial conversation. On one afternoon there he found that the young man he was chatting with was George Ellicott. George was his junior by more than twenty years, but his bright scientific mind was quickly drawn to the brilliant black man. George invited him to the Ellicott home, began to lend him books and journals on astronomy, and soon realized that Banneker was his superior, despite a lack of formal training. He marveled at the things Benjamin had achieved without even owning an adequate telescope, and it was not long before he gave him such an instrument. But it is said that for a time what drew them closest together was a handsome tall clock that Joseph Ellicott had made. It had four separate faces: One told the hours, minutes, and seconds; one showed the earth, moon, and other planets re-

Joseph Ellicott's clock with different faces on its four sides. From the Smithsonian Institution's show "Taking the Measure of Time."
(The Smithsonian Institution)

volving around the sun; one had twenty-four musical tunes and played one each hour; and one showed the clock's internal wheelworks. According to neighborhood tales, it had only one slight defect: while each beautifully ornamented face did its own job perfectly, the four could never be made to work at the same time. Joseph had tinkered with it for years and had now almost lost interest in making it work properly. There are different accounts among descendants about who first suggested that Banneker take a hand in attacking the problem. Some think Banneker himself dared to suggest this to the patrician Joseph. Others believe young George and Benjamin, looking at the clock pensively, both burst forth with the happy idea of working together to find the answer.

In either case, three months of ardent labor followed. Banneker came to the house several times each week and took the problem home in his head at night. It is not unlikely that the farmwork was given short shrift on some days. At last, he came to George Ellicott one day saying that he thought he had the answer. They rushed to try this new arrangement and there was a triumphant scene among all the principals when it proved successful.

Joseph would not have been at all jealous if he was indeed trumped by this younger team. The Ellicotts didn't think that way. This was a family that did not even try to obtain patents on its inventions—the ones that were revolutionizing the flour-milling industry—because in one case, they felt that an employee of theirs really deserved credit for the idea, and in another case, they thought their device was merely an improvement of someone else's previous invention. There was no U.S. Patent Office at that time, but they could easily have obtained a valuable patent from the Maryland government. Instead, their basic feeling was that inventions should be extended freely to anyone who wanted to put them to good use—that they themselves would benefit enough from the general increase in prosperity the devices promoted. Somehow, this open-handed philosophy made them richer. And with that same mentality, Joseph and George would have exulted over Banneker's contribution, and—as in the parable of the loaves and fishes—there was more than enough joy to go around.

What is certain is that as their collaboration increased, George and Benjamin studied books written by the two most famous astronomers of the day. Those two professors seemed to disagree with each other on the rules for determining what solar and lunar positions are needed to create an eclipse of the moon. After taking home the books by James Ferguson and Charles Leadbetter and making his own calculations, Banneker came back and told George—in his usual humble style—that both these great men appeared to have miscalculated. Again, George was determined that Benjamin should be recognized— neither because he was black nor in spite of it, but simply because he was right. It took some convincing by George to make Banneker write a clarification, which he wanted to pass around to learned friends. Benjamin thought it might appear rude or unseemly. But at last he did write a short piece, which can be found in his own journal and was also discovered and reprinted in the January 1863 issue of *The Atlantic Monthly*, then, as now, a leading intellectual magazine:

Commenting on Ferguson's *An Easy Introduction to Astronomy*, he wrote: "It appears to me that the wisest men may sometimes be in error; for instance, Dr. Ferguson informs us that when the sun is within 12 of either node at the time of full, the moon will be eclipsed; but I find that according to his method of projecting a lunar eclipse, there will be none by the above elements, and yet the sun is within 11 46′ 11″ of the moon's ascending node. But the moon being in her apogee prevents the appearance of this eclipse."

And referring to the second volume of Leadbetter's *Compleat System of Astronomy*, a separate Banneker memorandum pointed out a series of complicated "Errors that ought to be corrected . . ." (Later study showed that the two great astronomers were not entirely wrong. They had caused the conflict because one of them had made his calculation as seen from the earth, while the other, strangely, had done it as it would be seen from the sun.) The author of *The Atlantic Monthly* article, a very respected writer named Moncure Daniel Conway, added, "Both Ferguson and Leadbetter would have been amazed had they been informed that their elaborate works had been reviewed and corrected by a negro in the then unheard-of valley of the Patapsco."

Later, George Ellicott and Banneker went on to master the more advanced Ferguson book, *Astronomy Explained Upon Sir Isaac Newton's Principles.*

~

Banneker's comeback was complete. His old good spirits had returned. His family found him ready to play with his little nieces and join in singing and playing his violin, though not too well, they chided. (Note that in a later century, Albert Einstein's enthusiastic fiddling drew similar mixed reviews from his colleagues.) There was not a sign of the mental letdown Benjamin had suffered. His original personality had reemerged for good.

At the same time, the material conditions of his life were improving. Banneker had been working to complete his own separate cabin, and now it was done. Robert J. Hurry, an archaeologist who has headed the quest for evidence of Banneker's home and lifestyle, tells of finding traces of two log homes on the site, with Benjamin's personal cabin (which he is believed to have erected himself) having been much better built than the earlier home that dated back to the family's first days there. It seems to have been worked on over a period of several years. His house rested on a continuous stone foundation, roughly 14 by 16 feet, and there was a relatively large storage cellar. Fragments found show, among other things, that the cabin's occupant used ceramic ware of the most modern type for its day.

Hurry's findings also indicate that Banneker had a more varied diet than first presumed, and that more of it was purchased rather than farm-raised. Until the mid-1770s, neither Benjamin nor Mary, his mother, bought much meat from any store. It is clear that Mary was an industrious and saving person, and while she lived, the farm produced pork, beef, chicken, eggs, honey, vegetables, and grain. Later on, as Banneker dedicated himself more to astronomy (and when his mother was no longer alive to press him), he frequently bought pork from the Ellicott store, while still doing enough farming to raise some corn, vegetables, and fruits. The archaeological findings also showed pipe smoking to have been an intensive activity, but this tapered down as the years went on. The time around 1750, when his father was still alive, showed smoking to be at its height. Perhaps even his grandmother, Big Ma-Ma, was a pipe smoker. Later on, although tobacco purchases were moderate, a total of several hundred kaolin pipe fragments were found in the ground under the old cabin site.

~

Banneker's spirit was now so high that one of the great ambitions of his life took shape in his mind: to write and publish an almanac. He had some idea of how astronomers created the principal pages, which were called an "ephemeris"—an old word that was much more common then than now. It is a chart showing where the moon, planets, and other astral bodies will be in the coming months. Naturally, this was of special value to sailors as a way of determining their own positions, which was a life-and-death part of the seagoing life. While reading the latitude was relatively simple, the way to determine longitude was a deadly puzzle at that time. As international trade and, consequently, long-distance sailing kept increasing, hideous accidents were proliferating. In 1771, a British flotilla misjudged its position and ran aground with a loss of four ships and two thousand lives. Almost every sailor remembered narrow escapes when his life had depended on pure guesswork. The crown offered a huge prize for any invention that would solve the longitude problem, and it was finally won by John Harrison, maker of that "other" wooden clock many years earlier. Improved time-pieces and the reflecting quadrant were gradually narrowing the problem, but they were still too costly to be used on most ships. Meanwhile, the primitive methods that sea captains had to use were utterly dependent on reading the heavens. So the ephemeris was a vital part—in fact the real centerpiece—of any publication that was courageous enough to label itself an "almanac." It was courageous because anything short of great accuracy could have had serious repercussions for some readers and been potentially fatal for those at sea. The weather forecasts that were included were not expected to be perfect, but the ephemeris had to be impeccable.

Benjamin had not the slightest idea of how one went about getting all the information or processing it in a way that would make it usable. He realized that he would probably need an even stronger telescope and other instruments to take the necessary readings. In other words, this hope of his would have to be called childish and of no account, except for the one astonishing fact that trumps all others: He actually went on to turn it into reality. Fanciful as it seemed at that time, distant as he knew it would be, he thought seriously of one day publishing his own almanac. To appreciate the enormity of this ambition, it is necessary to know what a daunting venture it represented even when some of the wealthiest and most educated persons in society attempted it.

Banneker had learned that almanacs were highly profitable because the potential audience went far beyond the sailing profession. They were a leading form of publication at that time, when the amount of reading matter was limited. For many families, these annual editions were the only form of printed material in the house. But he also knew that only a few talented persons even dreamed of producing one. Creating an almanac required a thorough knowledge of the complex relationship between the Earth, planets, and constellations. One had to compute the hundreds of entries for the basic ephemeris, include extensive details about the tides, try for intelligent guesses about clouds, rain, snow, and winds, and then make the whole publication enjoyable with original writing. Apart from the seafarers who bought almanacs for sailing information, farmers bought them for long-term weather forecasts, and many other people bought them for their interesting essays on a variety of subjects, homey or philosophical. Sometimes an almanac also included humor and even poetry. Consequently, only learned persons with an unusually wide collection of scientific and literary skills tried to write such an all-purpose manual. The ones that caught the public's fancy and sold year after year made their authors financially well off. It was *Poor Richard's Almanac* that had turned its creator, Benjamin Franklin, into an independently wealthy man at an early age.

Benjamin Banneker was possibly the only person of his race who ever aspired to publish an almanac. As humble as he was in manner, he was highly confident of his own abilities. Even with his rudimentary equipment, he was developing enough feeling for the relationships among celestial bodies to form the first tempting idea that was to become one of his steadiest aspirations. And although he felt unready to prepare an ephemeris at that middle point in his life, he had no doubt at all that he would one day master the art. What joy he must have felt to dream of freedom from the everlasting chore of raising tobacco. He had no wish to leave the farm, but rather imagined that he might earn enough income as an almanac publisher to let him hire two good farm workers. He had no thought of changing his frugal ways, only to be independent enough to have all his hours free for his own thoughts. To earn his living by studying the stars, forecasting the weather, and writing philosophical essays seemed so much like being paid to play that he didn't yet dare to tell anyone about this. He thought of it as his guilty secret.

~

None of these exciting thoughts should be taken to mean that Banneker's world was wholly satisfactory. The changes he saw around him brought both joys and problems, in the way that innovations so often create overlapping tides and turbulence.

So it was when the Ellicotts came to the Patapsco region. They were a model family in nearly all respects—fair and even-handed, creative in the world of business, inventive at finding new ways to tackle old problems, and wealthy enough to put their ideas into action. By proposing new crops to replace tobacco, they were bringing hope to Banneker and his neighbors that their ongoing concern about the condition of their land might be solved. But as so often happens, forces that bring prosperity to a community bring unwanted consequences as well.

Banneker saw that while life was better for him, a bad trend was at work in society. The conditions of life for a free black were declining. Decades earlier, when there had been only a few hundred blacks in the area, most decent whites had respected them, and many volunteer efforts to improve their education had been under way. The proportion of free blacks grew from one in a dozen around the middle of the eighteenth century to one in three about sixty years later. In other words, less than 10 percent of blacks had been free earlier, and in sixty years that changed to over 30 percent. Recent research also indicates that a considerable number of "East India Indians" had appeared in Maryland during this late colonial period, and the whites probably regarded them all as "black." One might expect these numbers to add up to political heft and better conditions. But, of course, free nonwhites had no political role at all and, as their numbers grew, their treatment began to worsen. The main reason was fear, which is at the base of most arrogant or cruel actions. White people pictured these free blacks as becoming more and more uncontrollable. When they heard of a few incidents of drunkenness or violence, they imagined that their whole social structure was crumbling and would soon be dominated by such unruly people. They rushed to make harsher rules that might stop the trend, just as crime statistics today cause politicians to win votes for proposing that more jails be built.

Always evaluating the various religions, as he did for most of his life, Benjamin noticed that even the Methodists, who had once joined with blacks in building churches where there was no color bar, began to turn away from mixed congregations. The number of schools and societies for the relief of the poor also diminished. Some did sound a warning. A Presbyterian minister named Samuel Knox was especially brilliant in pinpointing what would happen if some people were left in "slavish ignorance . . . while the sons of fortune and affluence go to one or two sumptuously endowed schools." But such voices were drowned in a surge of popular feeling that, strangely enough, was a perversion of something that had a well-meaning origin. With more and more talk of independence, long before the Revolution of 1776, people became more aware that good citizenship was going to be essential to maintaining orderly self-government. Instead of making sure that as many blacks as possible were given the upbringing that would make them part of the structure, they thought only of new restrictions—passing tough vagrancy laws, limiting blacks' right of assembly, even requiring them to have a permit in order to own a gun or a dog.

Also, within a few years, another negative trend emerged. Eli Whitney's 1783 invention of the cotton gin hugely increased the demand for slaves in the Deep South. Up to that time, the process of separating cotton fiber from the seeds had made the crop just barely profitable. But suddenly the gin made cotton such a bonanza that every planter wanted to increase his output to the maximum, and that meant a need for more slaves. The prices offered for them soared.

Banneker saw these ominous signs and worried about them. But his thoughts were now full of the wider interests that came with his new friends and greater access to books and equipment. He was not ready—yet—to turn his mind to the war on injustice that was bound to come.

Banneker has been called an "Uncle Tom," thinking mainly of himself, playing up to white people, and unwilling to use his talents to do anything for his fellow blacks. Based solely on the early part of his life, that would not be entirely untrue. But it might be somewhat unfair, for we are talking of a time when rebellion and outspoken attacks on the system were rare. The fact that a person is less than a superhero does not mean that he is a coward or a turncoat. As for the great friendship he struck up with the Ellicotts, two things must be remembered: first, that the Ellicotts were a family so devoted to the cause of equality that only a bigot would have shunned them because of their race; second, Benjamin was first and foremost a scientist. In George Ellicott, he had found someone with common interests. He did not befriend George because he was white, but because they spoke the same language. No one in his family or in the farm community around them could have known about these subjects.

That said, however, the truth is that Banneker long seemed uncommonly anxious to avoid being involved in the controversy over race. Abolitionist societies that had learned of his talents wanted to publicize him as an example that blacks were capable of more than physical labor. Banneker at first refused to be thrust into that role. Much as he abhorred the evil of slavery and scorned any form of racism, there was probably something in his Dogon makeup that made him reluctant to be involved in confrontational matters. This inborn feeling was even stronger than his respect for the Ellicotts; he stoutly resisted their urgings to let his accomplishments stand out publicly. One solid reason for this attitude could be that Banneker was realistic enough to know his ability was of an uncommon order; he may have thought it would distort the picture if clumsy publicity made it seem that all black people had his talents and were capable of being scientists. That could not be said of any race, and it would promote a form of reverse racism. But even without such a reason, it seems fair to say that Benjamin Banneker was, for a good half-century, quite reluctant to stand up in opposition to slavery. He was afraid of white hostility at the idea of a black genius, and especially of one who was widely publicized. He saw that as a dangerous—a potentially suicidal—part to play. It would take a nearly miraculous set of occurrences to push him into the front line.

7

Turning Night into Day

When the successive eras of history or furniture are tied to the reigns of kings or queens, some of them are labeled "transitional." In France, a commode with graceful curved panels in the upper part that are reminiscent of Louis XV might have the straight tapered classical legs that seemed to foretell the coming of Marie Antoinette and her husband. In that case, an antiques expert would call it "Louis XV–Louis XVI Transition." If the periods of Benjamin Banneker's life were named in that way, the years from the mid-1770s to 1790 might be called "Farmer–Scientist Transition."

During those years, he could also have been described as a "gentleman farmer" in the sense in which that term was used in Britain, where a number of the great landholders or London social figures were also scientists of the first rank. They were amateurs, for they had not studied the sciences in the course of formal education, nor did they pursue this interest for monetary gain. But some—the immortal Sir Isaac Newton among them—made major discoveries and became members of the Royal Academy. If Benjamin Banneker's mind and soul had been born in the England of that day, he would have fitted perfectly into that superb group. Or if born in modern America, he would be called a multi-aptituder or a Renaissance man.

Examples of that kind simply reinforce the plain fact that Banneker was qualified in every respect for a far fuller life and a greater exposure to fame. In reality, as is true of so many persons, the accident of birth made it impossible for his remarkable makeup to flourish for a full four decades. And then it required something of a miracle to bring about the transition to farmer-scientist in his forties.

It might seem that a person who spent all but a few months of his existence in a cabin on one single farm must have had a seamless life, not at all subject to such arbitrary subdivisions. But in fact, even if no breakdowns are made into the separate years of his studies with Peter Heinrich or the influence of someone like Joseph Levi, five very distinct periods marked his life: *Childhood*, until he began to have substantial responsibility for the farm; *Young Manhood*, until a tragic romance or total boredom created a mental crisis; *Hiatus*, when he was slogging wearily through his duties; *Transition*, when work with the Ellicotts brought a great surge of new interests; and finally *Grand Old Man*, when new ideas and activism brought him recognition and a respite from farm duties, although he was shadowed by the threat of physical danger.

With the transition wrought by the Ellicotts, Banneker had gone back to keeping a diary, and later he even titled one of his record books his "Astronomical Journal." This is one of the few documents which, by a lucky accident, escaped the fire that obliterated his cabin and its contents after his death. It was found in 1852 by a Quaker philanthropist named Moses Sheppard, who had the book bound in leather. He also had parts reproduced and distributed. Although earlier diaries were lost, it is clear from the entries of the 1780s and 1790s that the pages usually served multiple purposes—thoughts on astronomy and life in general, collections of humorous stories, shopping lists that carefully noted the prices paid for each item, a number of the arithmetical problems that he liked to compose all his life, and a great deal more. It is a touching experience to see that a page partly taken up with a very complex equation or a trenchant piece of philosophy would then be divided by a bold pencil line and followed by an almost childlike problem, such as the following:

A gentleman sent his servant with £100 to buy 100 cattle with orders to give £5 for each bullock, 20 shillings for cows, and one shilling for each sheep. The question is to know what number of each Sort he bought for his master.

Answer:

19 Bullocks at £5 each		£95
1 Cow at 20 shillings		1
80 Sheep at 1 shilling each		4
100	proof	100

One possible impression on seeing these schoolboy-level problems is that a man who had been so deprived of normal schoolroom experiences—however mature and advanced his thoughts might have become—had somewhere in his mind a longing to make up for what he had missed. A more prosaic possibility is that simple problems of this kind were representations of the unusual clarity with which he pictured cosmic happenings, and this, too, is typical of some great mathematicians in all eras. Apart from formulas and jargon, their tastes and language often seem overly simple because their thought processes may go straight to core answers when an ordinary mind would be using more words and flourishes while groping its way. And a genius may sometimes notice a significant principle in what others see as an elementary calculation. The ubiquitous name of Albert Einstein serves as an example again, for he said it was only because he was thinking as a child does that the theory of relativity occurred to him.

Like the traditional British gentleman-scientists whom Banneker resembled, he included biological observations in his writings. Rather late in his life, he recalled his youthful experiences with seventeen-year locusts in this way: "The first year I remember was 1749, when I was about seventeen years of age, when thousands of them came to eat and destroy the fruits of the earth . . . I therefore began to kill and destroy them, but soon saw my labors were in vain. I therefore gave over my pretension. Again in the year 1766, which was seventeen years after the first appearance, they made a second and seemed to me to be as numerous as the first. I then being about 34 years of age, I had more sense . . . knowing that they were not so pernicious to the fruits of the earth as I did imagine. . . . " Going on to mention other visits up to 1800, he wrote that "they, like the comets, make but a short stay with us," and therefore he counseled accepting their brief presence without a struggle. Besides, he said, with a burst of nature loving that not many would feel, "they must be very merry, for they are singing from the time they come on this earth until they die." In all of this, there is more than a touch of the injunction, often attributed to St. Francis of Assisi, to distinguish carefully the difference between what can be changed from what should be left alone. It helps to illuminate the sharply criticized part of Banneker's character that was discussed in the last chapter, namely, the appearance of quietly enduring America's mindless racism for the greater part of his life.

Being a regular beekeeper, he made a number of original observations on the ways these creatures organized themselves or behaved under duress. For example, he wrote, "On a pleasant January day, I observed some of my honey bees to be out of their hive. Upon examination, I found that they had evacuated the hive and left not a drop of honey behind them." This mystery had to be investigated and thought out for the possible information it would yield about the lives and habits of the departed bees. Whether correctly or not, his finding ended this way: "Then on the 9th day of February, morning, I killed the neighboring hive of bees on a special occasion and found a giant quantity of honey, considering the reason, which I imagine the stronger had violently taken from the weaker, and the weaker had pursued them to their home, resolved to be benefited by their labour or die in the contest." The last passage is noteworthy as evidence that Banneker was hardly ever content to record an observation without drawing from it some conclusion about how the world works. The arsonists and other enemies of freedom who would later try to obliterate all signs of this man were right in fearing that he might serve as a role model to prove the abolitionists' conviction that blacks were "capable of intellectual effort." Using his intellect in the most complete way possible was the be-all and end-all of his life.

The practical items covered in the journal, although often on the same pages as astronomical findings, were mere notations, clearly separated from the subjects that demanded thought. They were in the same book because journals or even sheets of paper were costly and there was no room for waste in the Banneker budget. In one instance, he wrote in the journal: "I saw some condensed particles of the atmosphere of divers colours gathered round the moon, and that which was foremost near to the center appeared white, the second of an orange, the third blue, and the fourth red, nearly coloured like the rain bow. This small circle was in width about seven times the moon's apparent diameter."

Then, because there were a few lines left on the page under that, a line was drawn, and the following practical note was inscribed: "November 30th, Planted 170 pare tree sprouts."

On the next page, there was a long list of purchases from Ellicott & Co., with prices shown in pounds, shillings, and pence. Typical items are:

Thread
Flannel
Linden
2½ yards of sheeting @ ³/₉ per yard
A pair of shoes   1 shilling, 3 pence

There was nothing haphazard or scatterbrained about this apparently casual journal. The items were all carefully separated and clearly identified. And the entries dealing with the sun, moon, planets, and stars far outnumbered all the rest. Moreover, the journal provides evidence of a disciplined strategy for studying certain astronomical subjects in sequence, taking up aspects of the moon intensively for a time, then shifting to a different part of the heavens. As late as 1800, when he was nearly seventy, he wrote in a New Year's entry, "This year, in obtaining the planets places, I shall keep with the addition of 12 days, according to the method prescribed by Ferguson, but I had like to forget the Sun and Moon had only 11 days added to the old stile."

The cryptic lines and occasionally incomplete sentences should not be seen as evidence of imperfection in Banneker's writing. Many of these jottings were hastily made for his own purposes, and they are useful in showing the span of his daily interests. But they are not at all typical of his epistolary style, which became beautifully polished in his middle years.

Among other things, these journal entries add up to a sure sign of how firmly Banneker's thoughts were fixed on his long-term ambition to publish an almanac one day. When that time came, he would have to include humor, wise sayings, and even such homely items as prescriptions for curing common ailments. All these came naturally to him, as if his life had been a preparation for the multi-aptitude task of almanac writing that lay ahead.

Mary, his mother, the neighborhood expert on scents, essences, and home remedies, was one of her son's main sources for practical advice. She earned extra money for the family by charging small sums to those who could afford to pay. Banneker, always absorbing knowledge from every source, had made notes on her "Recipes for Curing Worms in Children and for Whooping Cough." And those would appear in his almanac.

The jokes he entered in his journal seem simple now. That is almost invariably true of humor from past eras, which seems to show that the onset of sophistication as a civilization ages requires people to work harder in order to achieve the laughter that came easily in an earlier century. Banneker's levity was well received when he tried it on the reading public some years later. Here is one example found in his journal:

> A very melting sermon was presented one day which caused all the Congregation to weep, but one man. This attracted the notice of people, and after the sermon they inquired why he did not weep as well as the rest of the Congregation. He pertinently responded, "I do not belong to the parish."

But it was astronomy that dominated Banneker's thoughts and the journals that he kept for the rest of his life. Every month in all those years includes information on lunar phases and eclipses. On that latter subject, he often indicated where they would be visible and especially how they affected the Baltimore area, no doubt because that city was going to be a big market for him if he ever got to publish an almanac. The phrase "This will not be visible in Baltimore" occurred frequently. On one occasion, the entry read, "Four [eclipses] in number during the year," then added, "one is invisible in Baltimore, while another [will be seen] from the Meridian of Baltimore and Latitude 49 South."

Along with such relatively routine observations are comments referring to cosmic thoughts he had enjoyed turning over in his mind for many years. Few pages from the past are as beguiling as Banneker's memoranda that mingle shopping lists with thoughts that deserve a place in the history of astronomy. And the sense of his increasing dedication to the world of ideas, as opposed to the routine, comes through forcefully.

However, he did not stop being a farmer at this point. He was a firmly practical man who was only temporarily distracted from the need to keep control over the farming activities, for he always remembered his father's admonitions. He had long since accepted the help of his sisters and their husbands whenever they could take time to lend a hand, but they were living in separate homes of their own, and their help was sporadic. Besides, Benjamin was the sole owner and always thought of the farm as his own primary responsibility. But there was a real change in how he approached this and even the kind of work schedule he kept.

It led to one humorous side effect. He worked at his telescopic observations much longer into the night and the early morning hours than he had ever done in his youth. And because his energies were somewhat diminished, he intentionally slept on much later into the following day. Consequently, there was more than one occasion when a white neighbor came calling to consult him on a crop question, found his door locked, and saw through a window that Banneker was still asleep when the sun was high in the sky. Some snide comments began to make the rounds of the neighborhood: "I never thought it of

Benjamin, but he's just another lazy black—lying there asleep when I've been working my acres for three or four hours."

The truth was that when Banneker rose late, he would then stay at his farm toil several hours later than usual to make up for the tardy start. It was far from an ideal arrangement, but especially in summer, he could do that until the light had faded, have time for some supper, and then turn to astronomy when the darkness was intense enough for five or six hours of good viewing.

His wiser visitors made it plain that he always seemed to be at work. "I never came to see him that he wasn't either laboring on the farm or standing inside the cabin, bent over the work-table that was covered with books, instruments, and lots of papers," said one person from Ellicott & Co. who often came with a message from George Ellicott or sought his opinion on a technical problem.

Probably Banneker's fear of getting into an even harder work schedule was what made him delay a shift from tobacco to wheat in his crop selection. Because of the friendship that had formed, it must have been embarrassing for him to keep planting tobacco while the Ellicotts were strongly urging area farmers to change to grain and so many were being won over. He was convinced that it was the right thing to do but uncertain of how much time the conversion might steal from his precious astronomy. Also, his innate conservatism made him wary of the financial hole he might dig if his inexperience with wheat caused a crop failure for a year or two. He did make the great shift a little later, but it was for a reason far greater than farm economics.

8

The Unfinished Revolution

For a good many months before the middle of 1776, Benjamin Banneker was taking a rapt interest in the possibility that the colonies would try to break away from England. Such talk and the fervor that went with it was somewhat lower key in Maryland than in neighboring Virginia, but Banneker's newspaper reading and frequent conversations with the alert Ellicotts made him far more informed than average. Neither of these sources, however, was correct in its opinion of what the rupture of transatlantic ties would mean to African Americans.

Perhaps this intellectually brilliant man was still politically immature and naive at that time. Or it may have been that unduly optimistic thoughts on the part of the abolition-minded Ellicotts had unbalanced Banneker's judgment. Whatever the cause, nothing about his life is clearer than that as 1776 approached, he genuinely believed the American Revolution would bring freedom for the slaves and a new status for all blacks. There could be no other rational explanation for the attempts that Banneker made to take part in the war effort.

As soon as he read the Declaration of Independence and learned that the colonies had come together in military rebellion against the British crown, he began trying to learn whether he could serve in the military. The negative answer he received was based on his age—he was about forty-five—rather than his color. It was probably a dishonest answer, or at least an ambiguous one, for Maryland's law on the subject was unclear, while a nearby state such as Virginia ordered free black men between twenty-six and fifty years of age to join the militia. The truth was that nobody knew what to do when a black person offered to serve in the military. Everybody in a leadership role, from state governors to the lowliest member of a city council, was in a near panic about how the blacks, slave or free, were going to react to the war.

There was a genuine fear of slave insurrection, for one thing. It was not at all imaginary. The belief that Africans accepted their humiliation and subjugation with very little opposition is a bad distortion of history. Because most Africans were normally good-natured, retained an inherited instinct for courtesy, and often gave affection to whites who showed themselves to be relatively kind, there has been too little notice of the courageous resistance mounted by some even in the face of ghastly punishments. A violent outbreak in New York, which was suppressed only after considerable bloodshed, had made an impression all over the country. The message it sent to people in government was that ever more stringent rules were needed to suppress and discipline these violence-prone blacks, whether slaves or free. The stark message for individual white slave owners was that they could be living on a powder keg.

These African people were theoretically mere property, like any other chattel, yet they were property that could move, have a sudden rush of anger, steal a gun and use it against a master, or drop poison into the food of a mistress. What kind of life was it to be surrounded and dependent on people who had good reason to hate you? Or at least good reason to resent the relationship, even when the master was actually kind? Such a decisive personage as George Washington was baffled and conflicted over the problem. As he confided to one of the few friends he trusted totally, Henry Knox, he genuinely believed that slaves should be gradually freed, educated, and integrated into society. He and Knox—who had done "impossible feats" for him in wartime—were trying to devise a way to start a model community of that kind with some of Washington's own slaves, but his tangled financial affairs never permitted it. He felt guilty when he freed some of the slaves, knowing the provisions he made for their support couldn't ensure as good a life as they had been used to. Worst of all, partly because Washington's mental faculties were slipping in his last years (by his own admission), he was unable to work out the financial tangle that left Martha a deadly legacy—some 150 slaves to be freed after his wife's death. He has been unfairly targeted for this, but in fact he did try desperately to avoid leaving her with servants who might have had a powerful reason to want her dead. How could she know whether there might be one among these pleasant people who would make the guaranteed freedom come true in short order? She didn't wait. Except for aged slaves who begged to stay, and some who legally belonged to relatives, Mrs. Washington wisely, and at great personal expense, quickly freed them all.

If whites had to be that frightened in peacetime, what did slavery mean to them in wartime? Each state tried to find its own answer, but often the many localities within a state took different courses. Even where there was no great fear of black insurrection, some whites were concerned about losing their "property" if slaves escaped and ran to the British forces, for the enemy had issued a proclamation promising full freedom to fugitive slaves.

The dilemma brought many diverse experiences. Interestingly enough, the first American casualty of the pre–Revolutionary War period was probably a black man named Crispus Attucks. In what came to be known as the Boston Massacre, Attucks was one of a boisterous crowd that encountered eight men from the British 29th Regiment in March 1770, on an evening when resentment was already brewing. He is believed to have swung a stick in a way that knocked a grenadier's gun out of his hand. The soldiers panicked and began firing, killing five civilians and wounding six others. Attucks was the first fatality. While this may have been an incident of little significance, the first military engagement of the Revolution, the battle of Lexington and Concord, on April 19, 1775, included a black man whose important role is well documented. This was Peter Salem, who served in the Framingham company of minutemen, having been given his freedom by the Belknap family so he could enlist. He went on to fight at Bunker Hill, along with several other blacks. Another African American whose heroism was attested to in a petition signed by fourteen Massachusetts officers was Salem Poor. They said he behaved not only as an excellent soldier, but "like an experienced officer, and the reward due to so great and distinguished a character, we submit to Congress."

This early use of blacks did not set a consistent pattern. In all, it is believed that about 5,000 black soldiers served in the army of the Revolution, chiefly because the Northern states were beginning to show more anti-slavery sentiment in the midst of a fight for liberty. That was not the case in the South. There was fear that the army would prove to be a refuge for runaway slaves, for one thing. Most masters did not want to give up their valuable "property," even when the military leaders were desperate for soldiers of any race. This conflict was sharpest in Southern areas where there was a real shortage of soldiers, and yet plantation owners resisted Northern entreaties to let male slaves serve. At the outset, George Washington took little interest in the issue, but he became increasingly anxious to see blacks recruited as the shortage of troops became acute.

By March 1779, Congress recommended to South Carolina and Georgia that they "take measures immediately for raising three thousand able-bodied negroes." Congress even named a brilliant young officer, John Laurens, who was an aide-de-camp to General Washington, to go to South Carolina and enlist local support for the recommendation. He was the son of Henry Laurens, president of the Continental Congress, and he had written to his father from Valley Forge, "A well-chosen body of 5,000 black men, properly officer'd to act as light troops . . . might give us decisive success in the next campaign." But even though British troops were menacing the lightly defended state, South Carolina rebuffed Laurens's repeated pleas. By 1781, Nathanael Greene, one of Washington's best generals, warned South Carolina that she would never forgive herself for the loss of her lands if they remained in British hands because of a refusal to let slaves take part in the defense. When that failed, Laurens wrote to Washington saying that the voice of reason had been "drowned by the howlings of a triple-headed monster, in which prejudice, avarice, and pusillanimity were united." The people of Georgia reacted just as negatively as the South Carolinians did.

Many thousands of blacks took the opportunity to flee, as the enemy British were urging them to do. Some blacks were employed by the British as laborers and found that the promises of freedom were honored. The British General Alexander Leslie felt obligated to take them along on shipboard when his troops were forced to evacuate, and as many as 14,000 may have been taken to England in this way. But for many who chose this means of escape, it was an unhappy decision. Some were enslaved again by new British masters, especially officers who went to serve in other parts of the world. Those blacks who got to England and avoided a new enslavement too often ended as miserable panhandlers on the streets of London, where the status of slavery was very vague, perhaps intentionally so. (There had been a legal case in 1772 wherein Lord Mansfield freed a slave on the narrow issue that his master could not force him to go into a foreign country. Mansfield thought this weakening of a master's rights was akin to ending slavery, but opinions on his interpretation were divided and there was no hurry to enforce it.) Estimates of the number of slaves in England at the time of the American Revolution range from only 3,000 to 15,000, and except for the limited number of dedicated abolitionists, few saw it as a pressing problem.

In America, meanwhile, the large number of black persons who might have affected the course of the conflict made black attitudes a major concern. In the chaos of war, the combined total of slaves who escaped to the British or went to live with the Indians devastated the labor supply for some plantations. When some rebellious slaves took up stolen arms, it became all the more questionable to consider trying to mold such men into an anti-British fighting force. Even in the cases where a former American colony considered ordering free blacks to form a militia, a county sheriff sometimes refused to let arms be put into the hands of men who had no good reason to be "patriotic" or "trustworthy."

Banneker harbored no ideas of turning against the American side—just the opposite, in fact. For the first time in his life, as far as we can tell, he saw a light at the end of the racist tunnel, saw a movement run by leaders who spoke of equality in the way Banneker had always thought of it. The practical nature that had prevented him from striking out against slavery when such opposition had seemed utterly pointless now was ready to fight because he thought a real chance was on the horizon.

Patient endurance had seemed the only appropriate way before. Now it appeared that the best chance for concrete action was at hand. This most peaceful of men was asking for a chance to fight. When that was denied, he looked for other ways to take part.

Banneker learned that the armed forces had a great need for more clocks and watches. In one more sign of his commitment to a cause that he thought would free the slaves, he actually left his precious farm in the care of his sisters and went to Philadelphia, where a leading watchmaking firm—one report says it was a shop owned by Esop Hernandes—employed him for a brief time. It is believed that only a few months passed before he heard a fellow worker say the war effort required food more than anything else, with grains heading the list.

According to one account, he asked himself, "What am I doing here? I could convert my farm's plantings to wheat, just as the Ellicotts have been urging me to do, and that would be more of a contribution than timepieces." Joseph Ellicott and his sons had expanded their operations to bustling Baltimore, which had broken away from reliance on Annapolis and now had its own customshouse. Their wagons made daily runs, carrying not only flour, but also a stream of information between their Patapsco base and the waterfront wharf they had erected in Baltimore. They were supplying French and Continental troops with flour along much of the East Coast. The supplies of wheat they received from nearby farmers had increased dramatically, but they would, indeed, welcome more—and certainly from their friend Banneker. So he quickly returned to the Patapsco Valley and began a hasty round of digging and replanting a new and unfamiliar crop.

Is it likely that Banneker did all this to help sustain a home-based tyranny that would keep some blacks in slavery and even the freed blacks in a second-class and insecure condition? It is surely right to think he was absolutely convinced that the stirring words "all men are created equal" meant just what they said. To imagine that the leaders who signed on to those words—at the risk of their own lives—were frauds would have seemed truly absurd. Or to think, in a more subtle way, that those leaders might become conflicted men who saw the dilemma they had created, but feared that trying to free the blacks would wreck their new nation before it had a chance to gain strength—this would have taken a political prescience that Banneker lacked. Nor, in all candor, could even the most advanced political scientist have foreseen what a group that included such diverse characters as Thomas Jefferson, James Madison, Thomas Paine, Patrick Henry, and Alexander Hamilton might do, for some of them went on to be intense political enemies.

What actually happened during those years was the chaotic jumble that generally characterizes war. Over 100,000 slaves are thought to have left the thirteen states during and after the war, including a fraction who were allowed to join the army. The South lost about 65,000, two-thirds of the total number, and the region, of course, was severely damaged by the loss of so many slave laborers—a damage it would feel far more strongly eighty-five years later when the Civil War ended. But the slaves themselves suffered the worst, for the hazards were daunting. Most who fled into the western wilds died from hunger or disease. Many who escaped to Canada froze or starved to death. A great many thousands went to the Caribbean, mainly to Jamaica, but many of those were snatched by new British masters.

Some slaves who had lived in the North had been promised their freedom if they enlisted in the Continental Army, and that promise was largely kept. Some, however, had to keep petitioning for up to ten years before getting satisfaction. Some states gave bounties to black veterans, and some gave pensions of up to $100 a year, which was significant money at the time. But most benefits required knowledge of how and where to file applications, and many never learned how to collect. Virginia gave some of its ex-slaves grants of land in Kentucky and Ohio, but only a few accepted the offer, preferring to live in a state they knew.

The horrid plight of blacks in general, so far worse than his own situation, had been gnawing at Banneker for some time. In his four decades of life, their condition had worsened dramatically as the growth of the black population kept leading to increasingly drastic laws intended to formalize slavery and keep stricter control of its victims. Maryland in particular had gone from being one of the more moderate states to one of the harshest. It had been settled twenty-seven years later than Virginia, and initially its relatively small plantations, growing mostly tobacco for export, had few slaves. In the mid-seventeenth century, only 3 percent of its people were black. By the time of Banneker's birth in 1731, many large plantations had been formed. Blacks had been brought from the West Indies at a great rate, and slaves were about a quarter of the population. The demand was so great that a young, able-bodied black man could be worth 8,000 pounds of tobacco (more than Banneker's father would pay for one hundred acres of good farmland six years later).

The white fears of black revolt had reached a high point at just the time when the colonists' fury against England was growing. That doubtless added to the fervor of Banneker's interest in the Revolution and his hopes that it would cleanse the colonies of this evil. But when the war ended in victory and the horror grew even worse, this became the one ugly stain that permeated the truly pleasant world of his scientific meditations. History does not record it, but it may be that he threw himself into measurements of the cosmos with even more energy as a way to escape the horrors he was hearing about. What had begun with a rule that a black person could move around only with a pass from his owner had become a set of laws about punishments that masters could inflict on an unruly slave or even on one who simply shirked his work. These laws escalated to a ruling that no slave could travel to visit another plantation, lest there be a conspiracy to start an insurrection; and it was decreed that any person who saw such a visiting slave could "inflict corporal punishment as he sees fit." Although there were laws that sought to keep a measure of balance in the rise of terror—rules about the number of hours worked and having free days on Sundays and holidays—these were dwarfed by legalization of punishments that disfigured the person, such as branding and cutting off ears. These were not rarities—they were commonplace, in fact. In the nation created to institutionalize equality and justice, many men and women who had dared to show a little spirit were missing one or both ears. Some, usually after an accusation of rape, had been castrated. A master could go as far as to inflict torturous punishments that caused the death of a disobedient slave—legally. Hearing of these barbarities doubtless played a big part in causing some of the violent dreams that Banneker described in his journal.

He was too fair-minded to think these excesses represented the views of all whites. He recognized that there were many people who thought totally differently in his state and even more in states to the north. State and local anti-slavery groups had sprung up from Massachusetts to Virginia. A Maryland Abolition Society had successfully petitioned the state legislature to soften certain laws for masters who wanted to free their slaves. Two other Maryland groups, the Chestertown Society and the Choptank Society, had a variety of projects to educate black children and teach useful trades and well-mannered behavior to adults. In Waltham, Massachusetts, a slave named Felix Cuff who had served in the armed forces during the Revolution took the Massachusetts constitution literally where it read "all men are born free and equal." He got a group of slaves to join him in declaring that they were all legally free. They fled from their masters' homes and hid in a cave called Devil's Den under Snake Rock. When chased and attacked by a posse headed by one Lieutenant Hastings, they beat the posse back, then raced to the village and managed to present the court with a paper asking for the prosecution of Hastings for having violated the state constitution. Astonishingly, popular sentiment turned out to be sympathetic to the rebels, and the court ruled in their favor. The state as a whole did not immediately outlaw slavery, but Cuff and all his associates retained their freedom.

Points of light like these helped greatly to prevent Banneker from becoming totally embittered or from falling into depression again. But he was reluctant to join with abolitionist groups that wanted to publicize him for their laudable purposes. As a sensible man, he knew the limitations and risks for one person living alone in a cabin and subject to fatal attack if his existence appeared to threaten the whole institution of slavery. There were several times in his life when his journal mentioned strangers firing what he took to be warning shots outside his windows.

Banneker's belief at this time, in the aftermath of a revolution, was that no crusade could have much effect on the wild trend that was being spurred by economics, supported by politics, and exacerbated by fear. (In fact, the strong-arm ways of the anti-abolitionists caused all three of the well-meaning Maryland societies to collapse suddenly between 1798 and 1800.) Although he had been naive about politics during the war, he soon began to think more clearly about the tangled affairs of the new nation and its differing views of slavery. While taking into account the problems the leaders would have faced in tackling the issue head-on, he thought they had missed the best moment for declaring an end to slavery. It would really have been easier, he felt, to abolish the hideous practice immediately at the time of victory, while a glow of satisfaction might have softened the anger of the slave owners. As the victory of 1781 became nearly a decade old, he recognized that his belief in the founders had been betrayed. But he tried not to give way to his furious disappointment too soon, still hoping that a great decision on the issue would finally emerge.

To any observer, even his loving sisters, Molly and Minta, or the ladies of the Ellicott family who admiringly noted and later wrote about his "noble and gentle manner," he seemed perfectly placid. They didn't suspect his anger and disgust at the realization that his race, instead of sharing in the new nation's great victory, was in for even worse times. Nor could they have known about the descriptions of violent dreams that have been found in his journal, dreams that must have been reflecting the barbarities he was not yet in a position to protest.

9

Attracted to the City

Some of Banneker's admirers think the Ellicotts are given too much credit for his accomplishments, as if having received help from whites would lessen the great significance of his amazing career. Such a conclusion would never have clouded a mind as balanced as Banneker's. Like any person who keeps his thoughts focused on real objectives, this man knew that using whatever advantages present themselves is common sense. And he was well aware that he had had far fewer opportunities than a well-born white person would have had; getting assistance, at last, when he was in his forties and fifties was only a small recompense for what he had missed earlier. It might have been called destiny's own "affirmative action."

On the other side of the coin, detractors have implied that Banneker's abilities were slight and that his reputation depended on being "puffed up" by the Ellicotts. Even if there were only the example of the wooden clock, this would clearly be false. For although the clock was a minor accomplishment compared with his thoughts on the universe, it was stupendously inventive of Banneker to have converted the principle of a watch into the dimensions of a clock (and then to have used wood as the material without knowing that such a thing had ever been done). All this took place more than two decades before the Ellicotts came to Maryland.

The idea that "no man is an island" applies to education more than any other aspect of life. Benjamin Banneker was, indeed, what we casually call a "self-made man" if ever there was one. He showed this by having the innate wisdom to learn from his grandmother, his parents, the Quaker schoolteacher, and the very few other contacts that brought new knowledge into his very restricted life. The Ellicotts noticed and admired him only because he had already made himself an outstanding person long before they came to his region. He would seem less wise if he had let any form of prejudice bar this friendship.

～

For the normal life spans of his day, Benjamin Banneker was verging on old age in the 1780s. Yet his zest for learning was greater than ever. Gifts from George Ellicott—along with the massive old table that became his treasured workplace, new books on astronomy, and a number of fine instruments that included an improved telescope—made the cosmos as new to him as it was for twentieth-century astronomers when they began to see the astonishing pictures taken by the Hubbell space telescope.

One book from England, Gibson's *Treatise of Practical Surveying*, which was considered the finest text on that subject, engrossed him for weeks. At the end of that time, with no hands-on surveying experience other than simple practice around his own area, he felt that he had mastered still another skill. No experienced surveyor would have agreed with him, for this was a craft that was normally learned by tramping through virgin fields under the guidance of a veteran. But Banneker's unique study methods and fantastic memory enabled him to imprint the contents of a fat volume almost perfectly in his mind. Then, because he was able to quickly envision the key points and overall geometry of a practical problem, he could superimpose his book learning onto the situation before him. Just as he had once studied a watch and envisioned a large clock, he imagined that he could take Gibson's surveying lessons and apply them to almost any challenging piece of land. That assumption would never be fully tested, but whatever tests he did encounter, he passed.

There were many examples of the Ellicotts' great role in his development—and of Banneker's own unprecedented way of turning the raw materials they provided into pure gold. Without the new technologies the Ellicotts brought to Elkridge, Banneker might not have come out of his long depression. Without the telescopes and books on astronomy they made available, he could never have gone beyond his intuitive feelings and become an astronomer of professional stature. Without the surveying book, he would have known nothing about the subject and could not have gone on to the new future it opened for him.

In an encounter that typifies the Banneker–Ellicott interaction, George once gave him some new instruments that Banneker knew nothing at all about. The younger man came by with the package and, finding his friend away, left it with a note promising that he would soon return to explain all the intricacies. It was a busy period for George, and several weeks elapsed before he got back. When he did, he found something that he told his family was "unbelievable," even for Ben, as he usually called him. Banneker had mastered the whole apparatus and was already routinely putting it to use.

The huge effect that the Ellicotts had on Banneker's life can only be understood by realizing the extent of their energies and their operations. The many mechanical innovations they were putting into their buildings were a revelation to a person who had suspected all his life that the outside world had marvels he had never seen or heard of. Now the Ellicotts had brought glimpses of that wider world right into the Elkridge neighborhood. Unlike the farming life, where it took several seasons to assess the results of an improved technique, every corner of a mill or a factory held an invitation to suggest ways of speeding this process or improving that product. Arrange a few pieces of metal or a pair of wheels in a new way, start the motion, and presto—the result was visible. If it was a failure, well, change the angle, add two more bolts, and try it again. Just as the telescope George had given him showed Banneker an entirely different cosmos, the mills opened a new world that he could visit at will, touch the machinery itself, talk about with others.

For the first time in his life, Banneker was neglectful of his farm—not flagrantly, but in stealing several hours, two or three times a week, when an afternoon that should have been devoted to clearing, digging, or planting was spent in the mill area, watching new construction under way or talking about it with others. It was also the first time he socialized with anyone outside his family and a few black friends who lived nearby. White neighbors had usually been "friendly" when they waved in passing or when they wanted Banneker's help in reading a letter, but they were not really friends. A few words about the weather might be exchanged, not much more. Talk in the Ellicott store was different because construction watchers in all times and places are the same. The activity, its newness, its excitement, are great levelers. Anybody can give an opinion, and everybody noticed that Banneker's opinions were some of the most interesting, most of all to the Ellicotts themselves. Even the rather patrician Joseph Ellicott invited Banneker to his huge home to see the four-faced clock again, and more recent creations. Some still had bugs in their operation, and he was always happy to hear Benjamin's thoughts on how to eliminate them.

Friendliest of all, quite naturally, was young George Ellicott, a blend of youthful enthusiasm and mature responsibility. His daughter, Martha Tyson, recalled when she was very old that "There was an especial empathy between one of the younger members of the Ellicott family and Banneker. That was my own father, George Ellicott." And she did not want it to be thought that his extreme youth was the only reason for his easy rapport with the black man, for George, as his family recognized, was no ordinary young man. She said, "That he had much energy and capacity we may know from the fact that the present road from Frederick to Baltimore was surveyed and laid out by him when he was seventeen years old." George Ellicott, in short, was something of a prodigy as Benjamin had been in his early years, the kind of person who can easily be on an equal footing with elders.

Although astronomy was obviously the main interest that Banneker shared with George, there were others. English literature, in fact, had been one of the first subjects that made each of them feel that finding the other was a real delight. In that area, Benjamin was more like the student, while George was his mentor, for George had a great library, while Benjamin's exposure to literature had been terribly limited. Just as George had been almost disbelieving when he realized what a feel for the heavens Banneker had—with none of the advantages of his own reading and fine instruments—he was touched and endlessly admiring when he noticed how much vocabulary, sense of style, and depth of ideas this phenomenal older man had somehow distilled from the few books he had read. To George, who sometimes tried to share his knowledge with reluctant friends and neighbors—and even gave lessons on astronomy to the girl he courted (successfully, at that!)—the friendship of a person with

Benjamin's appetite for learning was precious. When George's increasing duties in the family business got in the way of frequent meetings with Banneker, they exchanged more and more notes on their thoughts and experiments. Banneker would come home and find a new science book on his table, with a comment that raised a question about some chapter. He would usually attack the subject at once, pore over it until late into the night, then compose a return message to be delivered without delay.

It must be said, however, that the relationship between the two men was not totally equal. Just the fact that Banneker seems never to have addressed this youth as anything but "Mr. Ellicott," while George soon began calling him Benjamin and even Ben, is enough to tell us that they did not see themselves as equals. Whether this stemmed from a racial consciousness, it is certain that class or status made a difference. Maybe this is inevitable when one man lives in a mansion and is in a position to give great gifts that the other cannot possibly reciprocate. This does not denigrate the Ellicotts, but must be recognized in order to understand Banneker's situation during most of his life. Even men who freely admitted that he had a greater intellect than their own talked with him as if they were standing on a little higher ground than he was. That they genuinely respected him cannot be doubted (for bear in mind that Martha Tyson said she wrote her own book partly because "My father had long projected writing a memoir of Benjamin Banneker, but because he was always burdened by so many business duties, he died before he got to it"). Yes, there was genuine respect on both sides, but theirs flowed slightly downhill. All his life, even after he became nationally known, Banneker would accept this with no sign of rancor. He knew he was superior; this other matter he really regarded as "their problem."

❧

As the improvements at the Ellicott mill continued at a great rate, Banneker, in a sense, found himself at the cutting edge of the Industrial Revolution. The operations at Ellicott's Lower Mills had a frame coal house, a sawmill, a stone mill house, and a stone storage house. By using the advanced ideas of Delaware inventor Oliver Evans, who had authored an acclaimed handbook on mill building, they had automated their own mills in a way that sharply reduced costs. The effort helped to make Baltimore, which became their shipping port, a leading center of the flour industry. They soon had the largest and most automated mill in the country, all powered by a waterwheel. And a visit to this model operation became a regular stop for European businessmen who came to America. "Patapsco Flour" was a trademark known the world over.

Along with industrial development came the creation of a new town called Ellicott's Mills. The reputation for success had attracted more industries—ironworks, wagon parts and brakes, furnaces, wrought-iron utensils. Banneker was especially delighted to see that immediately after constructing housing for their workers, the planners set up a splendid school for the children of the entire area. The finest teachers were brought in to staff it, and there was no limitation at all on attendance. Nothing exists to show that the stiffening attitude of whites against free blacks had any echo in this case. In a very modern way, the local property owners were billed to share in the costs, and the children of the poor were as welcome as any others. The contrast with his own meager education might have given Banneker a pang, but there is no evidence of it. Among the ideas that he and the Ellicotts had in common was a genuine delight in progress. Banneker saw the school not only as a great thing for the children, but as a major step into the future. In his mind, he was still as much a student as the youngsters in the classrooms, and his enjoyment of the town's increasing tempo was genuine. That pace increased further when Ellicott's modest store became a general store of such size and reputation that shoppers from as far as Baltimore and Washington made excursions to see its shelves filled with fine imported products.

The birth and expansion of Ellicott City, as it came to be known, was a godsend in Banneker's life. His mother, Mary, had died in the late 1770s. She had expanded her activities beyond compounding herbal medicines and fine scents to running the boardinghouses that the Ellicotts and other new companies had set up for their workers until permanent homes could be completed. Even in her last years, neighbors marveled that Mary had retained the fleet-footed ability to race after a chicken and catch it without assistance. Now the death of all that vitality left a vacuum in the community, and it made a hole in Benjamin's heart. While still in his late forties, Banneker was hit by the feeling of old age that comes when all parents and grandparents are gone. He saw his sisters and their offspring regularly, and at least one of his nephews went to work for the Ellicott Company and stayed with it all his life. But his greatest solace, apart from his own studies and solitary thoughts, came from the vibrant town life that had sprung up so near him.

Seeing the well-preserved historic center of Ellicott City in the present day makes it easy to imagine how exciting the lively town must have seemed to a man who had so long looked down from his hilltop home and seen only a handful of houses and a general store. Today, even when most of the population has moved out to far-flung houses and apartments, and when the usual scattering of malls and fast food shops are mostly away from this center, the narrow old main street still bustles with activity. Stores, offices, and the gaggle of cars fighting for metered parking make it easy to imagine what it was like when horses and wagons went through the same exercise and then to think how that attracted the lonely man in his cabin some 1,500 feet above.

That elevated location of the Banneker farm is now called Oella, Maryland. But Oella was not incorporated until 1808, two years after Benjamin's death. In his day, it really had no official name. If asked where he lived, he would have said, "Oh, around Elk Ridge" or "Above Elkridge Landing." But it always needed a preposition, because neither of those town names applied. With the coming of Ellicott City, although this name still didn't extend up to Banneker's little mountaintop, its magnetic attraction certainly did. Even when his friend George was increasingly busy, entrusted with more of the family's management duties, Banneker was tempted to mount a horse and go down the road leading to the bustling city.

Everyone who saw him on such forays remarked on his excellent appearance. His looks were very much altered from the slim spear-like figure of his youth. He looked a bit older than the upper forties of his real age, heavier-set, with a very short neck and his head seemingly set right on his shoulders, causing one Ellicott employee who saw him often in the store to say that he looked very much like the revered Benjamin Franklin. Ladies often spoke of him as a fine-looking man, with his graying curly locks always carefully combed and his dress more formal than that of most of the men, as neat as if he were going to church.

His purchases grew more sophisticated—more shoes, finer fabrics, glass, and tableware. His diet included more meats purchased in Ellicott City, in contrast with the self-sufficiency that he and his mother had formerly maintained. Being busy with astronomy, he did far less livestock farming and bought even more pork. Archaeological exploration around the area of his old cabin shows that the diet of corn, vegetables, and fruits was fortified with considerable amounts of purchased fish and meats. In addition to being a customer of the Ellicotts, Banneker also had two other types of business affairs to talk over with them. First, he was one of their suppliers, as his farm produced respectable amounts of wheat for sale to their flour mill. Second, using his instinctive adeptness with numbers, he began discussing the possibility of trading bits of his land for cash at appropriate times when he might get a good enough price to afford more purchases at the increasingly attractive store. Recent studies show that he did later make some land trades of this kind, but always very cautiously, for he was conscious of how much land he would need to provide for his own upkeep, however long his life might be.

As he moved toward playing a larger part in the business affairs of the community, it now appears that he had a greater political interest than had been previously imagined. His sister, Minta Black, testified in court a few years after her brother's death that he had been accorded many of the rights of a free man, beyond merely being a property owner. Unlike most free blacks, she said, he had been allowed to give evidence in court cases even where white citizens were concerned. And she swore that he had voted in elections. The surprising degree of respect that was accorded to him at a time when the attitude of many Maryland whites toward free blacks was decidedly suspicious or antagonistic leaves an enduring portrait of Banneker's natural dignity and its effect on those around him.

10

Meanwhile,
at Mount Vernon

He was fifty-nine years old, thinking of Ellicott City as the outer limit of his excursions into the world, when, in July 1790, the Congress of the United States took an action that would give Benjamin Banneker a challenge and a prestige that no other black American had ever known. Almost exactly fourteen years after the start of the Revolution that had disappointed Banneker so sorely, Congress handed George Washington the sole power to choose and create a permanent national capital. The general made the most of it. He hardly needed to consult anyone. Within weeks, he announced the choice of a site that can virtually be called his and his alone—a choice that would lead to the dramatic turn in Benjamin Banneker's life.

It would be an understatement to say that President Washington's decision about location was not popular. Indeed, there were moments when a groundswell against the revered leader's choice seemed possible. The Constitution specified the size of the projected federal city, but not the location, for there was too much disagreement on that point. Most Northern political leaders, even while knowing the capital had to be outside of any state, hoped that the necessary land could be carved out within easy reach of some cosmopolitan center, such as Philadelphia, New York, or Boston. The sounds of surprise and dismay that came from all those who now faced periods of trying to live on the chosen site on the Potomac and Anacostia rivers were only partly genuine. The area was swampy and humid, but that was part of the generally accepted wish to have a capital very close to waterways and to the sea. Another frequent complaint reported in historical accounts, that this was a deserted area, did not stand up to scrutiny either. No state would have allowed a developed part of its territory to be amputated for separate federal use. And in a country with many wide-open spaces at that time, what sense would it have made to build a new city in a spot that would require massive clearance of existing properties? Actually, there were a good many houses around the chosen area, but they were widely separated by open fields and ditches. The fact that residents were few greatly lessened the cost of buying up private landholdings, a key consideration, since the government's funds for this purpose were truly meager.

It is understandable that the new nation's officials and their families were disappointed at the idea of moving to a fledgling city so far from the established centers, but they should not have pretended to be startled, for they might have guessed that something in the neighborhood of this little peninsula between Maryland and Virginia had been in the general's mind for a very long time, perhaps for decades. And once he was given the authority to choose, no one was capable of seriously challenging his decision.

There are reasons to believe that long before the states had united to the point of having a Constitutional Convention, before others had decided that a separate federal capital, independent of any state, would one day be needed, George Washington had secretly fixed on this specific location as the place where he hoped to see a new city. The first President himself appears in an entirely new light when viewed as the subtle planner who worked for years to situate the national capital where he wanted it. And there is firm evidence of a campaign to make this into a reality as early as 1785. How he positioned himself to accomplish it shows that beyond being a courageous and farsighted military leader with an iron will, he was a patient and adroit strategist of the first rank.

To work toward winning his way, he used an array of talents that are seldom combined in one human being—a keen judgment of other men and the approaches that might appeal to each one, a sharp sense of money's role in most human affairs, an ability to keep his thoughts close to the vest while listening patiently to the contrary arguments of others, a well-veiled killer instinct for turning their inconsistencies into deal-makers, and even the employment of social graces and small interludes of good fellowship to soften or mislead the opposition. It is clear that he used his temper to intimidate anyone who might be thinking of crossing him, but it is less well known that he was sometimes willing to use an engaging friendliness if it were needed to win others over.

Not quite as accidentally as it seemed at the time, Washington had arranged to be in several brief meetings with leading merchants and landowners of Maryland and Virginia in the years following the Revolutionary War victory. While he was being hailed in every one of the former colonies, he devoted most of his time to being a Virginian and to his near neighbors, prefiguring the modern dictum that "all politics is local." At one of these postwar gatherings, the general surprised half a dozen men of varying prominence by suggesting that they come to Mount Vernon for a few days to discuss matters of common interest. All were surprised, and the two youngest were stunned by the honor. Because Washington's aloofness had long been a trait that kept others in awe, when he chose to lift the barrier briefly, the result was seductive. Now he used a show of warmth and informality to ignite a positive glow. When the group, casually assorted as it seemed, arrived at his home on March 28, 1785, their mood could not have been more receptive.

Adding to their amazement as they arrived, what they saw was not the imposing giant whose majestic bearing alone inspired compliance. They found the general in coarse farm-worker's clothing, standing in a field to one side of the home as a soft rain fell. His shoes were mud-caked, and water dripped from his broad straw hat. Welcoming them warmly, he told them to go in and find Mrs. Washington, while he would go and get properly dressed.

He must have felt considerable irritation that Robert Morris, one of the richest men in America, had sent word that he couldn't come, for Morris's holdings in Pennsylvania, New Jersey, and Delaware would have meant that an even greater region was represented. But he didn't betray his chagrin at all. To the five who were there, he gave the impression that nothing could please him more than spending a few days in their company. They were Colonel George Mason and Alexander Henderson, both of Virginia, and three Marylanders, Samuel Chase, Thomas Stone, and Major Daniel Jenifer. The last two were younger men of promise, unused to such elevated company, and a little awkward at first. And while the short, plump Chase, a wealthy Annapolis merchant who was known for his stormy ways, would have been ready to start talking business at once, even he went docilely into the drawing room to take tea and make polite small talk.

As the days went on, the other five men meeting around a table on the second floor could not have been oblivious to the fact that General Washington, at 6'3", was a head taller than any of them. But he was so gentle a discussion leader that Chase occasionally stomped a big foot to emphasize a point, and the much younger Stone, Henderson, and Jenifer found the courage to speak their minds. As for George Mason, he was invariably direct and plainspoken, a trait Washington prized. In the end, they all found themselves pretty much in favor of what seemed just a set of general ideas about trade in the region and how the waterways should be used. Simple as it appeared, they were doing no less than laying out a development plan that would govern investments and population movement far into the future. In a period when each state was jealous and suspicious of every neighbor, such thinking was revolutionary. Since it just so happened that all five of the visitors were members of their states' Houses of Delegates, one of them proposed that their thoughts be put on paper as the informal draft of an agreement. Washington, almost diffidently, said that in order to have it done by three persons from each state, he wondered if they would like to count him as a third Virginian representative. All the others were overcome at this graceful condescension and one said, "Every state would be honored to have the Hero of our nation speak for it in such a way."

And so it was that six relaxed comrades, sipping ale together in a cozy Mount Vernon room, agreed on a virtual treaty of trade and navigation for a big part of the mid-Atlantic region. The key element was the Potomac River. In a day when states (and even some private owners) thought of waterways as prize possessions, with travel and fishing subject to tolls, this agreement proposed that the Potomac would belong to no state, would be a toll-free highway and open to fishing by all. (When it came time to choose a national capital years later, should it have been any surprise that a site on this unique river came first to mind?) Samuel Chase, in fact, saw it as being a model for all, saying, "The truth is that making everything open and free is the way to build this nation. I'm a merchant, and I can tell you that we only tie our hands when we try to charge fees and duties every time some goods go from here to there. The more we share and trade, the more good fortune we promote for ourselves." It was to take Europe 165 years to start experimenting with this bumptiously American route to growth—the idea of a Common Market that enabled a few colonies to populate a continent in a matter of decades.

There was no dissent from that, either. In fact, General Washington said—and it's fair to imagine that he had a faraway look in his eyes—"There is so much business and new interest in this region that I have heard land prices up and down the river are rising every day." Was he thinking, even then, of where the money would come from if a new nation burdened with massive debt from the recent Revolution had to find sufficient cash to buy land for a new federal city? It would be difficult enough if all thirteen states were willing contributors to the war debt. But the southerners denied that they owed any part of it; the Northern states had made the decision to go to war, and the debt was largely theirs, as the South chose to see it.

Two years later, at the 1787 Constitutional Convention in Philadelphia, came the discussion that greatly displeased three major cities—Boston, New York, and Philadelphia itself. At one time, they had taken it for granted that one of these three would become the nation's permanent capital. But they were undercut by the memory of a frightening incident. Years before, while Philadelphia was serving as interim capital, troops of the Pennsylvania militia had menacingly surrounded a meeting where the early national fathers were debating controversial issues, including the matter of back pay for men in uniform. These soldiers thought they would get their money by holding the lawmakers hostage. It had been a comic-opera scenario, and the founders had escaped to a New Jersey site. They came back only three months later, after Pennsylvania's legislature promised that such mutinous behavior would never be repeated. But the nation-builders had learned a lesson: There must be a federal capital located outside of any state.

At the Constitutional Convention, a size of three miles square was first proposed. But South Carolina's Charles Pinckney kept pushing to triple that figure, explaining privately to some of his colleagues, "The big northern cities are sure to keep trying to get the capital back if we set up just a small federal city. It's got to be big enough to show it is permanent." And in the end, Pinckney won his way. "Ten miles square" was written into the Constitution.

Fortunately, less successful was one founder's suggestion that the Constitution should impose a limit of no more than 3,000 men to defend the federal area. George Washington, on hearing it, whispered to a young member of the Convention, "I will make no remark on that. But you should move to amend the motion to say, 'No foreign enemy may invade the United States with more than 3000 troops.'"

But there was no agreement whatsoever about the capital's location. The North continued to feel that its undisputed seniority in urban matters must certainly bring the capital its way. For that very reason, the South was equally determined that such arrogance must be put down. Consequently, the U.S. Constitution had to be finalized without naming the whereabouts of the federal capital. It was left open to further discussion. The impasse continued for three years more, until June 1790, when three men of great prestige—Secretary of State Thomas Jefferson, Treasury Secretary Alexander Hamilton, and James Madison—met with several key congressmen in New York City. The clever compromise they worked out used another problem—the old war debt dispute that George Washington had worried about five years earlier—as a lever to move the location question one step nearer to solution. No one could doubt that they had President Washington's prior approval when they struck the "dinner-table bargain," basically agreeing that a Southern location would be chosen for the national capital provided the Southern states would assume a share of the Revolutionary War debt.

Now came the question of just what "Southern location" it was to be. In only a month, the Congress passed the Residence Bill of July 16, 1790, naming George Washington the agent of Congress to choose the site—anywhere along a sixty-seven-mile reach of the Potomac—for a permanent seat of government. He was to acquire the necessary land and appoint commissioners to oversee construction. He had won full power to turn his old dream into a living capital city, to mold it with his own hands. Washington pretended to be almost reluctant to accept so great a responsibility alone, but he quickly overcame this hesitation, for was this not the moment he had planned for years? Only weeks elapsed before he announced his choice of a site. It was obvious that he could, in fact, have done so the next day, for within hours, he had a group of prechosen assistants fanning out over the area, posing as private buyers and paying cash for the land before its future federal use drove up the prices.

The area of destiny—the new Federal District—was that small peninsula next to both Maryland and Virginia, between the Potomac and Anacostia rivers, that Captain John Smith had seen while sailing the Potowamacke in 1608.

The announcement was a bombshell. Not because it was truly remote, for it was adjacent to the neat tobacco port of George Town, Maryland, and quite near Alexandria, Virginia, which was then the nation's third largest port, but because it was far from cities where the future officials wanted to spend any substantial part of their year. They would go on complaining about the "primitive conditions" for many years, but it was nonsensical to have agreed on the need for a new city and then pretended that it should have been born fully developed.

Fortunately, the Father of the Nation could seem unperturbed by the complaints. With all he had done to create a country, he need not—and did not—feel the least bit apologetic if his choice was unpopular. He appeared sure of being right. This man who, when learning to be a surveyor at age sixteen, had once told his diary that "the bed as they call'd it was nothing but a Little Straw—matted together and one Thread Bare blanket with double its Weight of Vermin such as Lice and Fleas" was hardly sympathetic with those who found the new capital's accommodations distasteful. Having pushed his way through so many overgrown and marshy areas while learning his trade, he saw nothing daunting about the site. Moreover, it was not many miles from his own Mount Vernon estate, which he was continuing to improve. He had, in fact, often ridden near the selected land on his way to George Town to clear his tobacco shipments through the customshouse. That very familiarity and proximity, of course, created scandalous tales, tales he probably never heard—of how rich he would now grow by having used his power to select a spot certain to increase the value of his own nearby properties. The rumors found an eager audience, but they had little or no impact. Most Americans really felt that there would have been no United States if George Washington had not put every bit of his mind and body into such a desperate cause. In all the ways that really counted, their faith in him was total.

Washington made the official proclamation of the new District of Columbia on January 24, 1791 (with no mention yet of the city's name), and he directed the survey of the ten-mile-square area to go forward. At the same time, he also appointed three commissioners to oversee the design of the city: Daniel Carroll, Thomas Johnson, and Dr. David Stuart.

The usually taciturn President was uncharacteristically wordy about the new city and its prospects, perhaps as a safeguard against the continuing efforts of Boston, New York, and Philadelphia to win reconsideration for their own dwindling claims to become the federal capital. Even such a grim event as the yellow fever epidemic of 1793 was used by some promoters as evidence that the chosen capital was ill placed, citing a figure of 6,000 dead there—clearly spurious, since the capital under construction had a population only in the hundreds, and the deaths were few. Health records for the time are very inexact, but historians of the Centers for Disease Control say that Philadelphia, the temporary capital, was hardest hit that year, losing over 5,000 persons, or more than 10 percent of its population—and a third of the population fled the city. The President feared that he might cause even greater panic if he left Philadelphia for a planned vacation at Mount Vernon, and Mrs. Washington refused to leave without him, so they stayed on heroically, but quite safely, because a temperature drop had killed off the mosquitoes that, unknown to medical science, were the carriers of the disease.

Even after this, Washington was soon writing letters like this one to Arthur Young, a British agricultural reformer, on December 12, 1793: "The Federal City is increasing fast in buildings and rising in consequence; and will, no doubt, from the advantages given to it by Nature and its proximity to a rich interior country and the Western Territory, become the emporium of the United States." More than once, he roundly predicted that the new city would "quickly rival the great capitals of Europe." That turned out to be very far from the mark, for the city's population stayed well below expectations for a full half-century.

George Washington would, of course, not live to see how slowly the city of his dreams would move toward the global position he envisioned. In the immediate aftermath of his choice, he had less grandiose and more irritating matters to plague him. He hated the office of President, made that plain more than once, and was so infuriated by the political maneuverings of others that he secretly began to question his own abilities for the first time in his life. This dislike for the office probably contributed to his lackluster performance as an administrator. Two of the presidential decisions he soon made in an uncharacteristically offhand way regarding the building of the capital city—although they were not of great national consequence—were embarrassing examples of his declining effectiveness.

11

Astonishing Choices

After so much strategic brilliance in winning the right to choose a location for the capital city, George Washington put himself into a box when it came to getting it planned and built. He hastily chose a quarrelsome Frenchman to design it, which created animosity on the part of many American architects and Northern political leaders who backed them. Then, trying to calm those critics, he chose a fine surveyor with perfect American lineage to lay out the city's basic lines, but failed to scent a possible surprise when he went along with the man's insistence on selecting his own staff. In both cases, he was employing a great talent, but creating situations that would haunt him.

In choosing Pierre L'Enfant as chief architect, the President took on an impossibly difficult man who laid out a magnificent plan for the new capital. But it was far too grand for the city's role at the time and hopelessly beyond what the young government was able to afford. L'Enfant had a feeling for the city's destiny and a dedication that justify calling him a great early Washingtonian, but his vision was a full century ahead of his time. Only George Washington himself shared it, and it is said that his eyes sparkled whenever the young architect spoke. Yet this junior person was one of the very few whom Washington found hard to handle, and L'Enfant eventually made the President miserable.

The small Frenchman's daring and unflinching courage were what had appealed so much to General Washington during the war years. More than anyone else, he became a protégé of the great man. As the son of a court painter in the time of Louis XV, Pierre L'Enfant had studied under his father at the Academy of Art at the same time that he was being trained as an engineer. He was the quintessential multi-aptituder, with a splendid future before him in his own country. But he was captivated by the new nation being born across the ocean, and at age twenty-three he came to America as a volunteer and was commissioned a lieutenant in the Continental Army. He was absolutely fearless, a glorious wartime trait that proved self-destructive when carried over to civilian operations. He had survived the terrible Valley Forge winter with the general, was wounded at Savannah, captured by the British at Charleston, then released in 1782. The admiring General Washington saw to it that L'Enfant was honored by the Congress and made a Major of Engineers before his discharge into peacetime life.

In that same year, L'Enfant began to use his artistic talent to good advantage, creating stage sets for a Philadelphia pavilion. But with his usual flair for making quick moves, he was attracted to New York City and soon began to get commissions for private architectural projects. He was earning good money from these and from a number of memorials and church buildings that he planned.

By 1788, when New York celebrated its adherence to the new U.S. Constitution, he had designed a massive domed banquet hall to seat six thousand guests. That feat made him the natural choice to convert New York's old City Hall, making it into the first Capitol of the United States. It was renamed Federal Hall, and George Washington was inaugurated President there on April 30, 1789.

That proved to be the apogee of L'Enfant's thriving career. In the next year, soon after the President had chosen the site for Washington, D.C., L'Enfant wrote to his old commander and offered his services in planning the new capital city. No one could have known how badly he was overreaching in his notion of what was expected of him. Although his greatest fame was just ahead of him, his life went downhill from then on. Perhaps the thrilling grandeur of his letter to President Washington should have sounded a warning note, but instead, his old general was enthralled by it. L'Enfant had written: "To change a wilderness into a city, to erect and beautify buildings . . . to that degree of perfection necessary to receive the seat of government of so extensive an empire." Except for that last word, the President was thinking along similar lines at that time, so much so that some think he had once been tempted to accept a crown and make the new nation a constitutional monarchy. He had the good sense to suspect that those who urged this were interested mainly in the titles of nobility it might mean for them. But Washington always found L'Enfant's dynamism infectious, and he answered the letter promptly, making him the chief architect of the city.

In doing this, Washington committed an oversight that might seem astonishing for a military man accustomed to precision about chains of command. In truth, Washington not only hated the office of President, but felt he lacked the skills needed to be a civilian administrator, and was subject to the whims and jabs of politicians around him. Before taking office, he had written to his trusted friend Henry Knox, "My movements to the chair of government will be accompanied with feelings not unlike those of a culprit who is going to the place of his execution." He found it worse than he had feared, and his hair went from a mixture of chestnut brown and gray to all white in less than a year. There were times when he lost his temper and ranted while several others were in the room. In a typical out-of-control moment, he shouted that, "by God, I had rather be in my grave than in my present situation."

In the case of L'Enfant, Washington had failed to make it clear that the chief architect would report to and be accountable to the city commissioners, not to the President of the United States. That was a fatal mistake for, incredibly, this general before whom the greatest and richest Americans became tongue-tied with awe was never able to make the younger man understand his place. Repeatedly, L'Enfant would run to the President with ideas or complaints about routine problems. And Washington could not bring himself to give the firm put-down that was clearly needed. This unique partiality that no one else ever had was so well known and even talked about among members of the inner circle that it would not be surprising if some of them made remarks about an improper relationship. But not the slightest evidence of that exists. A much likelier explanation would be that Washington had a touch of the francophilia that was current at the time. In most cultural matters, the French were being copied by the rulers and the elite of other nations. Americans have always pretended to disdain such a notion, but the more elevated an American was, the likelier he was to be touched by it. Given how Washington admired and was influenced by the Marquis de Lafayette, it is possible that even a mind as independent as his was not immune. Add to that a generous amount of gratitude for young L'Enfant's services, a warm feeling for his nearly filial attitude, and genuine amazement at his total lack of awe in Washington's presence—all possible factors in making a man who had no son of his own reluctant to destroy this charmed relationship.

For his part, L'Enfant apparently thought that as a friend of the President—who had shown himself to be highly favorable to the proposed plans—he had no reason to waste time arguing with other creatures who understood nothing of his elevated goals. His opinion of the feeble intelligences in this primitive land must have taken another dip when the newspapers referred to him as "Mr. Longfont."

Even before L'Enfant dug his own grave, President Washington was again encountering complaints from leading Northern cities about the preference that had been given to this foreigner. There were frequent reminders that since this was to be the federal capital for the Northern states, too, the fine architects of places like Boston and Philadelphia should be given at least an equal chance to contribute their ideas. The President, therefore, prudently hoped he might quiet this xenophobia by appointing someone from a respected old American family to handle the daunting job of chief surveyor, the one who would mark out the boundaries within which L'Enfant would create streets and suggest the locations of major buildings. This was, in fact, the easiest of choices for the President. As an old surveyor himself, George Washington judged Andrew Ellicott to be the finest surveyor in the country, and he handpicked him to define the boundaries of the city that would come to bear his name. Ellicott was a fast worker, which accorded perfectly with Washington's strong wish to see the new city take shape as rapidly as possible. He was from a fine Maryland family, which no Northerner could sneer at, and he had an excellent war record. In naming him, the President was sure he had picked a winner, and he saw no reason to cavil when Ellicott insisted on the right to choose his own staff.

Andrew Ellicott did prove to be a fortunate choice, for he was even forced to complete much of the work of the capital's original designer when the erratic and intemperate L'Enfant had to be fired. Ellicott went on to be the surveyor who extended the Mason-Dixon Line westward and marked out the Georgia–North Carolina boundary, and the line that separated Spanish Florida from the United States.

What makes Ellicott a key person here is that he courageously—some would have said outrageously—named Benjamin Banneker as a principal assistant in the historic survey of Washington, D.C. This was a truly startling choice for Ellicott to have made. He might well have expected a backlash of anger from other elite leaders. If challenged, he could not even have proved that the black man he chose was an experienced surveyor. He was simply going on his assessment of Banneker's talent and character. It happened that Banneker had studied the finest textbook on surveying; and with Banneker, one good book constituted a course. But Ellicott would not know whether his decision was a good one until they actually started work. President George Washington must have been thunderstruck to find an African American on the team, but he had promised Major Ellicott that he could choose his own staff, and he kept his word.

The task that Ellicott accepted was a tremendous one. Every other major city in the country had grown up naturally, generally from a few farmhouses leading to a general store and then other venturesome farmers and businesspersons clustering in the area until it grew from village to town to city. The District of Columbia would be totally different. Its four ten-mile lines had to be created from scratch, aligned and physically forced through woods, underbrush, rocks, and depressions—over swamps and even across rivers. And all this had to be done without taking any land from Maryland or Virginia beyond the exact amount they had agreed to.

Though he was self-confident, the major felt the need of a first-class assistant who could help him to resolve the myriad problems that were sure to arise and also be a strong right hand with all the highly technical questions. The caliber of person he wanted was shown by the fact that he first asked his nephew George to fill the job. Now thirty-four years old, Banneker's close friend George Ellicott was entrusted with much of Ellicott & Co.'s top-level management. His stature can be judged from the fact that anxious as he was to take part in his Uncle Andrew's historic project, George had to say no because he was heavily engaged in the expansion of several mills and did not dare take leave at just that time. But he had a firm recommendation to make, and one account says he quickly suggested, "Take Benjamin Banneker as your assistant. There's not a better man for the job anywhere."

It has been said that the major quickly agreed. But in fact, there were a few minutes of hesitation for discussion of a subject that has been touched only skimmingly, if at all, in most previous accounts. Quite surprisingly, in view of his moderation in all things, it seems that the Ellicotts thought Banneker had an alcohol problem. There is a memorandum written by the major indicating that he asked George Ellicott, "What about the drinking? Have you taken that into account?" And Ellicott is said to have replied, "I don't think that will be any problem."

The fact that this was an issue gains credence from a line that Banneker himself wrote in his journal at the time he accepted Andrew Ellicott's offer of the survey job: "I resolved that I would do no drinking at all during this time."

This subject of alcohol is touched on lightly in a few other comments by acquaintances, but it does not seem to have been a serious problem for Banneker. Drinking was probably not a lifelong habit, but one that he started only in later years when a little more leisure and a little more affluence had brought a relaxed attitude. The fact that his detailed lists of purchases make no mention of buying either wine or hard spirits seems to weigh against any sweeping assertion that he had a major problem with alcohol. But since the Ellicotts were so well disposed toward Benjamin in every way, the mere fact that this was discussed seriously at such an important time has to be taken as evidence that they had occasionally seen him showing the effects of overimbibing, as a few other friends had. Looking back at his life now, this comes, perhaps, as a surprise, but also provides a little relief at finding a small chink in the almost-too-perfect facade that he presented to the world. Maybe George and Andrew Ellicott felt that way about it, too, and only took it seriously at the moment when he was going to be entrusted with a historic responsibility.

At any rate, the Ellicotts made the decision in Banneker's favor rather quickly. Martha Tyson, the impeccable contemporary source, has mentioned this moment in a way that attempts to recall the dialogue as vividly as possible. In that version, Andrew Ellicott went at once to Banneker's cabin and told him, "Get your clothes together for a great trip. We're leaving in three days to help President Washington build a new federal city. My job is to survey the entire site before any building begins, and I would like you to be my assistant. Can you leave your farm for a few months?"

Even though he tried to appear outwardly calm as usual, Banneker's high excitement is evidenced by the fact that he thought of asking a woman's advice about preparing for the adventure. George's wife (and Martha Tyson's mother), Elizabeth, was the Ellicott woman he knew best, and one who held him in very high esteem. She wisely stressed warm things, which probably saved his life in some of the arduous months of primitive living ahead. Her selection was what he had with him when he and the major left on horseback on February 7, 1791. Their first stop was Alexandria, Virginia, the port city outside the appointed federal territory. It was the point from which they would begin to survey the area.

It might be said that a black man's historic participation in the building of his nation's capital city in the eighteenth century was an example of fate's totally haphazard ways. But a better argument could be made for the moral that destiny's dice usually favor the person who is well prepared whenever and however the game is played.

There is no doubt that others could have been found to handle Banneker's role in the survey of Washington, D.C., but his combined knowledge of surveying and astronomy would have been hard to match on short notice. The independent-minded Ellicott wanted Banneker as an assistant because of his competence, precision, and high sense of responsibility, regardless of what most whites might have thought. George Washington, astonished as he was, kept his promise and let Ellicott have his way, for he wanted to see the survey begun without delay.

The unique nature of the Ellicott–Banneker partnership was highlighted almost immediately when they stopped at a leading hostelry called Wise's Fountain Tavern. It was a proud old establishment that had long been called Fountain Tavern, and its recent new owner, Wise, was determined to maintain its reputation. The innkeeper was surprised to see this imposing man of military bearing riding up to his door with, as he thought, a fine-looking Negro "servant," not trailing behind, but riding side by side. Recording a conversation after more than two centuries is hazardous and should be considered only a verbal sketch of what transpired, but it is said that when Ellicott asked for two of his best rooms, Wise responded, "I have an excellent room for you, sir. But your servant will have to occupy a place in another part of the inn, of course."

"He is not my servant," Ellicott is believed to have said. "We are on an official mission for the government of this country, and we'll need rooms close together." As he usually did,

Major Ellicott got his way. Whether those words are correct or imprecise, the thought deserves an early and honored place in the spotty history of civil rights in the United States. As late as the mid-twentieth century, only a few white persons of strong character refused to dine at a Southern restaurant if it would not also seat a black fellow traveler. In this case, even if we have seen previous indications of a subtle line that made Andrew and even George sometimes talk to Banneker with a touch of condescension, the major was not about to allow anyone else to disrespect him. He was Major Ellicott's subordinate, as anyone else on his staff would have been, and thus a comrade whom the confused Mr. Wise would have to treat as an equal.

In the days ahead, as they set up a base camp, much as a mountain-climbing expedition might do, Banneker was regrettably forced to give up his comfortable quarters at the inn and move to a tent on the cold, damp campsite. The reason was that one of his indispensable duties was to take full charge of the astronomical clock, a device that ensured consistent time and positioning. Banneker understood now why he and George Ellicott were the first people Andrew Ellicott turned to in his search for an assistant. He may have recalled the afternoon when, as a very young man, he had stared in wonder at the first watch he ever saw. Now, uniquely skilled as he was in both watchmaking and astronomy, he could study this state-of-the-art device for a half-hour and understand the part it would play in establishing the precise outline of the District of Columbia, as set forth in the Constitution of the United States. It is not hard to imagine what turmoil, what endless arguments among politicians, could have been set off by some deviation that gave either Virginia or Maryland a reason to claim that one of the capital's boundaries had been slightly awry at one point and then, when extended for ten miles, robbed the state of hundreds of square miles of land.

To one who has never attempted surveying, it may seem superfluous to consult the stars before establishing lines here on Earth. But in Major Ellicott's case the challenge was almost like locating positions at sea. The area he was to set apart was largely in a wilderness where there were few established starting points. Staring out over brush and swamp, where so much looked alike, the danger of error was very high. The project's leader had to be a woodsman as well as a surveyor. And there had to be an astronomer working with him. Sightings that had been recorded on a previous afternoon could be taken up accurately on the following morning only if the exact placement on Earth was confirmed by the angles between those points and certain known stars. And since Earth's motion constantly altered those angles, the precise time of the measurement was vital. Since this could have been thrown off by small temperature changes, a delicate arrangement of several thermometers all around the equipment was also required. It was helpful that Benjamin had studied surveying. Although it was book learning, never strengthened by practice, it enabled him to understand everything that the rest of the team had to do. But his skill in astronomy was still more important. Not even Andrew Ellicott was as competent to make sure that each day's work would begin with points that had been confirmed by the heavens.

So Banneker often had to check the clock, with readings of the sky every hour throughout the night. He also had to keep watching and moving the several thermometers that ensured a steady temperature for the clock. Then, just when he was about to settle down for a little more rest, Ellicott, who pushed himself as hard as he drove the whole team, usually arose before dawn and rushed to the camp to begin consultations with his assistant. The cold ground and sleeplessness affected Banneker so much that he complained of feeling poorly in the frequent letters he wrote to his sisters.

His relations with the rest of the team were apparently excellent. The engineer corpsmen invited him to join them at their common table at mealtime, but he politely declined. It is plain that the invitation was wholehearted on the part of the other men, but Benjamin apparently thought it prudent not to risk any possible appearance of a wish to contest the color line. In keeping with the delicate sensibility that he may have inherited from Dogon ancestors, Banneker was particularly anxious to avoid anything that might make problems for Andrew Ellicott in the course of this historic mission. So he requested that a separate small table be set for him, but always in the same room or tent in which the others dined, and there seems never to have been a whisper of complaint on anyone's part. Incidentally, even when wine was being served at the main table, Benjamin declined the offer and held firmly to his resolution to avoid alcohol for the duration of the survey.

No account mentions actual encounters between Banneker and the President. It seems likely that Washington asked for these to go unreported, which must have been a most irritating position to find himself in—wanting to be recognized as a hands-on observer of the survey, yet pretending not to know the man who was doing one of its most meticulous jobs. It is virtually certain that Washington and Banneker were in the same meetings on many occasions. The President came to the Alexandria site repeatedly, staying at Suter's, another well-known Alexandria inn. And each time he arrived, Washington went quickly to the work area, checking the progress in detail. Banneker's technical part in the project would have made the old surveyor wish to question him personally. But although President Washington had approved (or rather, had not disapproved) Banneker's appointment, he seems to have wanted to avoid the kind of racist scuttlebutt that would certainly have caused astonishment in the North and anger in the South.

Washington limited himself to statements proclaiming that the work was going splendidly and that he was very satisfied.

The only newspaper known to have mentioned Banneker's race was the *George Town Weekly Ledger*, which called him "an Ethiopian, whose abilities as a surveyor and astronomer clearly prove that Mr. Jefferson's conclusion that this race of men were void of mental endowments was without foundation." The wording and the slap at Jefferson show that the liberal tendencies of our press go back a long way, even though the political leaders could more easily ignore its jibes then than they could as the media grew to giant proportions. There is evidence that a reporter from this same George Town newspaper asked the President about Banneker on one of his visits to the survey site. And, the story goes, George Washington turned on his heel and walked away without a word. He reacted in this way, from what is now known of George Washington, not because he objected to the man himself, but because he feared the South's reaction if the Banneker story was publicized.

∽

Thomas Jefferson, who was often mercurial in his thoughts about race, was different from Washington in this regard. He had written publicly about blacks' lack of intellectual ability. At one point, he pronounced them definitely inferior. But typically, he also wrote opinions casting doubt on that. In his capacity as Secretary of State, but also because he was the recognized authority on all matters of architecture and taste, Jefferson had been consulted about the appointment of Major Andrew Ellicott and had specifically given approval to his choice of an assistant. One account, in fact, says that "Jefferson encouraged Ellicott to employ Banneker for the preliminary survey." The term "negro" was not used, however, and it is likely that most lead-

Banneker and Major Ellicott in the field.

ers in either the North or the South, ready to pounce as they might have been, had no idea of who Ellicott's assistant was.

For over two solid months, Banneker was at work or on call virtually twenty-four hours a day. Many men on the project had harsher work to do, clearing trees and pushing through the underbrush. But all of them were free to rest when darkness fell. Only Banneker had to jump up after a few hours' sleep and make his astronomical observations. Then, after conferring with Andrew Ellicott at daybreak, he could try for a little more rest. But he was almost invariably called for more consultations all through the day as the chains were moved and new sightings had to be established. He didn't have to be told that he must remain in touch and ready at any hour. He knew it, for he understood perfectly what Ellicott's objectives and problems were. It would be a great mistake to underestimate Banneker's contribution to the survey of the new capital city just because he was on the job for only a few months. During that time, the basic layout was set. His role might be compared to that of the navigator on a large aircraft. He might not fly the plane, but his early calculations would affect the course of the entire flight.

～

Meanwhile, Pierre L'Enfant was accumulating enemies at a great rate. His disdain for almost anyone who ventured to advise or caution him on any subject caused head-shaking on all sides. For the most part, he simply ignored them all and went directly to President Washington to get differences settled. It is hard to imagine George Washington being timid, but on this subject he was really embarrassed, time after time, for he knew that L'Enfant's detour around proper channels should not have been tolerated.

Naturally, such a person would clash more than once with the strong-willed Andrew Ellicott, and he would have been especially dismissive of Banneker—not because of color, for the French have not usually been given to anti-black racism, but because he would think an assistant was beneath his notice. Banneker's renowned gentleness might have made him a useful intermediary, but there is no firm evidence of such a role. In any case, the disturbances between architect and surveyor did not lead to serious explosions because L'Enfant seemed to sense Washington's real admiration of Ellicott. Amazingly, that kept the Frenchman from pushing their disagreements too far.

Aside from the President, Thomas Jefferson was the only leader whom L'Enfant was willing to converse with almost as an equal. Here, he felt, was a person whose love of France showed at least a modicum of taste. He did not realize that Jefferson, for all his fascination with fine architecture, had become wary of the great plans L'Enfant was proposing. Jefferson could be so devious in conversations and correspondence that his true feelings were hidden from others. In this case, he warned the President that L'Enfant seemed to be projecting huge expenditures, far beyond anything the new country could afford. But at the same time, he tried to appear helpful to the young architect, even procuring detailed maps of the greatest European cities for him and models of beautiful buildings that might be used in making choices for the American capital city.

The one most openly concerned about L'Enfant's impractical ideas (and Jefferson's dual position) was Alexander Hamilton, the Secretary of the Treasury. Hamilton even contrived cleverly to interrupt L'Enfant's District of Columbia work by diverting his attention to a New Jersey project. But that, too, was a failure, and the delay was brief. The truth, however, was that President Washington's favoritism was well known, and the others could not shake L'Enfant's position. Not until L'Enfant did it to himself.

Constantly going over everyone's head and troubling President Washington had become an accepted fact of life. It is uncertain how long that might have gone on if L'Enfant had not committed one unforgivable piece of destructive arrogance. A home belonging to an important city official was being constructed on a site that the architect strongly coveted. It was blocking an avenue that he was determined to extend through that very spot. He kept insisting that the half-completed house be destroyed. The official, however, had powerful friends who turned down the architect's demand. This so enraged L'Enfant that when the family was out of the city, he had the place demolished. That was too much for George Washington, for a reason that will shortly become clear. L'Enfant was dismissed.

This story has been told before, but the importance of the victimized official, Daniel Carroll, has not been brought out. Carroll was first among the city's three commissioners and technically L'Enfant's direct boss. That alone would show that the destruction was "worse than a crime—it was a mistake," as an old French phrase puts it. But there was more to it than that.

The capital city did not yet have a name. The District of Columbia or the Federal District—these were designations, not true names. The question had come up but had never been answered. The three commissioners had been directed by the President to decide on a name for the capital city, but he was loath to press for a decision, lest it give the appearance that he was especially anxious about what name it was to be. Ironically, it was Pierre L'Enfant who had pushed them to make a choice. He contacted the commissioners (an odd act, since he seldom seemed to notice their existence) to ask what the name was to be. They met on September 9, 1791, and wrote him a response that should have been no surprise. It said in part:

> Sir: We have agreed that the Federal District shall be called "The Territory of Columbia," and the Federal City the "City of Washington".

The City of Washington. Of course. George Washington would never have proposed his own name for the capital. But the commissioners he had appointed could hardly have called it anything else.

So the person whose home L'Enfant had destroyed was not only his boss, not only the city's leading official, but the person whom President Washington was counting on to see that his old dream of an American capital located in his own area would be capped by bearing his name. Even in his ambitions, even in his political strategies, Washington was no ordinary man. Whatever he did was monumental, and he never looked for cheap or easy honors. This one, like all the others, was fully earned by hard and patient work dating back to the informal talks at Mount Vernon nearly a decade earlier.

More pliable and lesser persons took over L'Enfant's job, and some of his most exciting original ideas were quietly pushed aside. The man was never able to overcome the shock and depression this caused. For years after that, he was seen walking around town alone, sometimes nostalgically picking up bricks or pieces of lumber at a construction site, then looking into the distance, as though seeing the mirage of a great avenue or vista that should have been there. L'Enfant made a few attempts to restart his architectural practice, but they failed, some because rich persons who were about to give him a commission got warnings of how difficult and expensive he would be. The money he had made in his best years lasted for a time. At one point, he made a petition to Congress for $95,000 as compensation for the Washington plan he had created; after some years, he was awarded $3,800. But as he lived on to the age of seventy-one, he existed mostly on the charity of others. And when he died at a friend's home in nearby Prince Georges County, he was penniless. Some of the vistas he imagined and sketched are there now, arousing gasps of pleasure from foreign tourists and pride from Americans, for a century and a half later many of his concepts were revived by a much richer nation that had finally caught up with his vision.

The names of L'Enfant and Banneker have sometimes been coupled, as if they were co-workers or equal contributors in the building of Washington. Attempts to equate their roles are misguided. The former played a creative part in which he let his unfortunate personality overwhelm his brilliance. Benjamin Banneker, on the other hand, had a technical job that he did perfectly. It was far from being the pinnacle of his great career, but it perfectly illustrated how his lonely studies had made him ready for great opportunities when the moment came, and it opened his life to more accomplishments. It is unfortunate that his role was partly distorted and largely hushed up. He has existed in dim memory mainly on mangled ideas about his work, and even utter falsehoods that are unwise attempts to glorify a man who needs no such embellishment. Indeed, some Washington leaders of recent times—knowing almost nothing about the real Banneker—have made up sheer myths, especially whenever Black History Month has brought on a search for sound bites on radio or TV. A former member of the District of Columbia City Council once said on a leading radio station, "Too few people realize that Benjamin Banneker built the city of Washington brick by brick and stone by stone." Of course, he built absolutely nothing except his own cabin in Maryland.

There is also a much-repeated story that Banneker, having seen L'Enfant's original design for the city just once, saved Washington by recreating it all from memory after the moody Frenchman refused to let anyone have the original. This is less egregious than the brick-by-brick building story, because Banneker's memory was probably equal to the task. But thoughtful historians question the belief that there was really only one copy and that the whole plan could have been lost. It is certainly true that L'Enfant might have been spiteful enough to deny anyone the right to see his plan. In fact, there is a letter written by Andrew Ellicott on February 23, 1792, in which he stated, "In this business we met with difficulties of a very serious nature. Major L'Enfant refused us the use of the original! What his motives were, God knows." But then he continued, "The plan which we have furnished, I believe will be found to answer the ground better than the large one in the Major's hands."

It is believed that this substitute "plan which we have furnished" was made up from small separate renditions or drafts of the overall plan. There is no sign that continuance of the work

142

was seriously endangered, and it is highly unlikely that anything had to be done from memory. Ellicott and the new designers who replaced L'Enfant had a series of wrangles, but the project went on reasonably well. The letters that he and Banneker wrote home told of hardships, but they were mostly about health problems caused by the grueling conditions. The absence of the overbearing little Frenchman was such a relief that there was little worry about the shelving of his great ideas.

As Surveyor General of the United States, Andrew Ellicott received $5 per day. Benjamin Banneker was paid at a rate of $2 per day, which was not a handsome sum for those twenty-hour days he struggled through. But it was not at all racially motivated, for this was the stipulated rate for an assistant surveyor on this project. It worked out to the most he had ever earned for such a short period, but he was looking forward to much better paydays to come, plus something that meant more than money. He knew then, as he had known all along, that the doubts about a black person's capacity for intellectual effort were totally wrong. Still, as an old farmer, what a warm satisfaction there would be if he could prove the point by making his pen earn more than his plow had ever produced.

12

~~⌒~~

Back Home to Plant . . . and Publish

A fter more than two months on the Washington survey, Banneker began to feel that he could leave the team without jeopardizing the work. They had been hard at it all this time, working seven days a week. By late April, the basic lines establishing the new city's external boundaries were well along. The great accuracy of the astronomical clock was no longer a prime requirement, so Banneker's specialty and his greatest contribution to the effort could be dispensed with.

The capital city, as established by Ellicott and his team, was not going to be quite the exact square that the Constitution called for. It would be more like a trapezoid, with its southwest side having a length of ten miles plus 230.6 feet, its northeast side 10 miles plus 263.1 feet, its southeast side ten miles plus 70.5 feet, and its northwest side ten miles plus only 63 feet. That was as close to square as the topography permitted. But notice that all were 10 *plus*. None was minus. As minor as the differences may seem, it took the word of a person with Andrew Ellicott's prestige to make sure that any challenges to the delicate judgments he had to make could be rebutted. Sixty or seventy or 230 feet, when extended for ten miles, translated to a substantial amount of extra territory being taken from the two adjoining states.

Banneker was well aware that his role in laying out the nation's capital could have symbolic importance of value to the anti-slavery societies in many states. Up to that time, he had been disinclined to see himself used in such a way. In notes he wrote about his projected almanac, there were signs that his feelings about this were changing. He mentioned the possibility that such a publication could be used to support the abolitionists' cause, but he continued to be more concerned with practical work than with symbolism. In any case, the last quarter of a year had adequately taken care of both aspects. He was both a symbol and a practical example of what an African American could accomplish.

His own concerns, however, made him anxious to go home. It was a real feat for him to have lasted so long. At age sixty, he was suffering badly from rheumatic pains that may have resulted from the many nights during which he had lain for hours on damp ground outside his cabin, looking up into the sky through his first primitive telescope. Now he had been forcing this same aching body to rise before 5:00 A.M. in the chilly humidity of the D.C. area because he was the only man who was capable of operating the astronomical instruments. He was far from being the only sufferer in the group. Major Andrew Ellicott, although he was hardy and much younger, had written repeatedly to his wife that severe bronchitis was almost laying him low. And the harsh conditions were underscored by Ellicott's added reports of casualties among the men who had to clear underbrush and trees for a forty-foot lane along the whole forty-mile length of the new city's boundary lines. Within that lane, stone posts serving as markers had to be sunk a mile apart—or as close to that as possible in cases where one of them would have been in a swamp. Not surprisingly, "Another of our men has been killed by a falling tree," wrote Ellicott in one of his letters home.

Apart from the oppressive conditions, other reasons impelled Benjamin to take leave of his historic mission. The main consideration was caring for his farm. Banneker was not one to let prestigious work jeopardize his livelihood. Vividly aware as he was of the great honor it was to serve on this project, he had been writing regularly to his sister Minta, reminding her of the steps that had to be taken to clear and ready the ground for the 1791 crop. He knew she was a conscientious person who would do all she could. She let him know that she was pressing her husband, their other sisters, and their children to lend a hand. But they all had their own family chores to take care of, and the long-established custom of expecting Benjamin to bear the main responsibility for his acreage made it questionable whether they were really doing all that was needed. Even if there were no indications from persons who knew him, which there are, Banneker's diary entries that record his work schedule and other living habits indicate that he was always conscious of the words his no-nonsense father had said long ago: "Remember, it's the crop that puts food on the table. Do all the thinking you want, but only after the farmwork is taken care of." In a sense, Banneker was going through the pressures that all the country's farmer-politicians, even those as highly placed as Washington and Jefferson, felt when they let national duties keep them away from their estates. They, too, often complained in letters to friends that the crops were smaller and poorer when they could not be overseeing the work in person. But unlike them, Banneker would not let national duties threaten his finances, and he got Major Ellicott to agree that his services could now be dispensed with.

He headed happily back to his farm. All his aches seemed to have been lifted from him on the day he got back. Martha Tyson's nearly firsthand account, mostly gleaned from her mother, Elizabeth Ellicott, tells of his exquisite courtesy in making an immediate friendly call at their home, bearing a personal message from Major Ellicott, assuring the ladies that he was well and very happy with the progress of the work. "Mr. Banneker appeared to be full of joy at being back in his own community," she said. Later, when she was quite old, she repeated this to her own daughter, who was helping her to write her memoir, not about "Ben," but about "Mr. Banneker."

⌒つ

The farm turned out to be in better condition than Banneker had anticipated. That added to his high spirits, for it meant he could quickly complete the planting and turn his mind to the old ambition he had nurtured for so long. It was time to see if he could really be the first person of his race ever to prepare his own almanac.

The ephemeris of celestial computations had been started months earlier, before Banneker had left for the survey. This scientific part of the work was near enough to completion that Banneker had asked two Baltimore printers if they would wish to publish his almanac. They had turned him down, but politely and giving a credible, not race-related reason. He then tried a third printer named John Hayes, the only other one in Baltimore. An Englishman who had come south from Philadelphia, he was of abolitionist sentiments. He made an encouraging response, mentioning that before making a commitment, he would ask Major Andrew Ellicott for an opinion on the accuracy of the work. The final answer was delayed for so long that Banneker wrote a quite touching letter asking Ellicott to give a favorable opinion before it became too late in the year for the 1791 computations to be saleable. But Ellicott, too busy to even continue with an almanac of his own, seems never to have sent back any word on this.

When news came that Hayes had decided not to publish the almanac, it appeared that all his effort had been for nought, and Banneker felt, as any first-time author would, crushed. But, in fact, his luck had turned. Some totally unexpected good fortune was on its way to him from across the ocean. A young Quaker who had gone from Philadelphia to London and organized an abolitionist center there somehow heard about Banneker's almanac and alerted his old Pennsylvania friends to this opportunity for favorable publicity. The news came to James Pemberton, who had recently taken over the presidency of the Pennsylvania anti-slavery society from the dying Benjamin Franklin, and it was a timely reminder of the great propaganda value of an almanac written by a black man. Pemberton had already heard of the subject and had corresponded with a Baltimore businessman, Joseph Townsend, who had helped to found a Maryland society to promote abolition. In both states, there were a number of these dynamic leaders who took real risks and put their cause ahead of all personal considerations. In fact, one Marylander, Elisha Tyson, had become famous for personal bravery in rescuing captured blacks from slave ships.

Townsend assured Pemberton of his cooperation and put his business affairs aside to check the facts about Banneker's work. His hasty inquiries to the Ellicotts and to John Hayes led to a firm decision that they would all cooperate to ensure publication of the almanac. By then, it was already too late to have the work published for the 1791 season. A complete revision would be needed to get a 1792 edition prepared. But, of course, when the Washington survey project intervened, everything had to be left in limbo. All this, in addition to worry about his farm, had been on Banneker's mind when he went off to assist in planning the new capital city.

Now, back from the Washington survey, he began a very methodical program of getting facts and figures ready for a 1792 almanac, which would have to be ready for sale late in 1791. Consequently, even this version had to be done rapidly. Fortunately, Banneker had a new sense of confidence. The months in Washington being part of a professional team had made him much surer of his approach. He had learned a great deal from Major Ellicott about work methods and orderly project management. He even splurged to purchase a beautiful journal from the Ellicott store to keep his records, both celestial and terrestrial.

Final touches to the ephemeris were added within weeks, during which time he held to a new schedule—spending part of each night on studies of the sky and part of the next day on putting his findings into the new journal. Next, he began trying his hand at the essays, humor, and practical information that would round out the publication and give it the stamp of his own personality. It had to give readers a feeling of knowing and trusting the writer. He had long been able to fascinate listeners with his words of wisdom. Could he convey that same warm comfort to the printed page? Would the words of a black farmer appeal to an almost entirely white reading audience? What on earth could he and his readers have in common? Only when the work went on sale would that vital question be answered. But now, at least, he could proceed on the knowledge that he had many citizens in two states who would help with the great effort of finding printers willing to produce and distribute his little book.

Some of the printers who took an interest in the job had to back away because their regular clients let it be known that they would stop dealing with them if they were going to be in league with a black man. Now, however, the balance of power was on Benjamin's side. Those abolitionist societies that Banneker had tended to regard with mixed feelings were also good customers of the print shops. If James Pemberton or Joseph Townsend wanted them to print this African American's work, they would not turn away. Pemberton wanted just one more word of assurance that these calculations for 1792 were of good quality. He asked one of the most respected scientists in all the colonies, David Rittenhouse of Philadelphia, to review Banneker's ephemeris calculations. He could not have devised a sterner test.

Rittenhouse was old and near the end of his life. But there was no weariness in his answer. His response was meant to be enthusiastic: "I think the papers I herewith return to you a very extraordinary performance, considering the colour of the Author." It was more than good enough to delight Pemberton. Banneker was less easily pleased. He showed once again that despite his gentle and humble manner, he had a clear, calm confidence in himself. "I am annoyed to find that the subject of my race is so much stressed," he remarked. "The work is either correct or it is not. In this case, I believe it to be perfect."

In any case, the work that had nearly died unseen was quickly put into print. There were exciting moments when William Goddard, Baltimore's finest printer but a notably quirky man, first insisted on being the exclusive publisher. But he dropped the demand and then amazed everyone by sending a very cooperative and helpful letter to the Philadelphia printer who was preparing to publish. More excitement came when another handwritten copy of the whole work was needed at once in Philadelphia, and Banneker, who happened to be ill at the time, was only able to work slowly. But when it was done, heroic measures prevailed, with George and Elias Ellicott running a relay race to get the copy into the hands of a visiting businessman who conveyed it personally to Philadelphia.

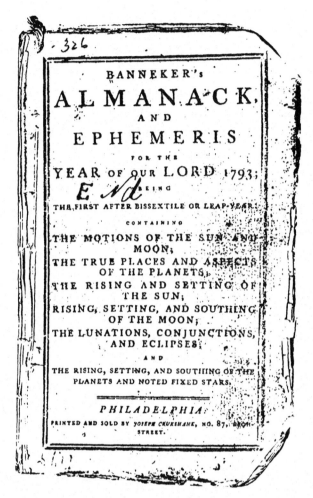

Cover of Banneker's 1793 *Almanack*. (Rare Book Division, Library of Congress)

Another providential turn of fortune helped to set the stage for a triumph. A Baltimore physician named George Buchanan addressed the Maryland Historical Society on the subject of great blacks who helped to prove how wrong it was to treat this race as inferior. The talk was a huge success, and it pointed to Ignacio Sancho, a writer, Phillis Wheatley, a poetess, and astronomer Benjamin Banneker as examples of persons of color who were advancing the entire *human* race. The speaker was specially commended by the Society, and his words were published, preparing the ground for the almanac as an event worthy of notice.

Just in time, in the last weeks of 1791, Banneker's 1792 almanac was on the market, announced to the public as " . . . a greater, more pleasing and useful Variety than any work of the kind and price in North America." It was distributed far more widely than anyone had expected: printed and sold in Baltimore, wholesale and retail, by William Goddard and James Angell at their printing office in Market Street; sold in Philadelphia by the printing firms of Joseph Crukshank and Daniel Humphreys; sold in Alexandria by the printers Hanson and Bond. The sales were large, and word-of-mouth enthusiasm kept them rolling. The identity of the writer, far from being hidden, was stated emphatically. The printers had long since stopped worrying about the supposed disadvantage of a work authored by a black man; they had increased the number of copies in their first run, wisely concluding that the racial angle would turn out to be a bonus.

"What on earth could he and his white readers have in common?" had been a question. And the warm answer came back: "Almost everything." Many persons bought it as a curiosity, and then marveled at its quality and told their friends that it was simply a fine almanac, regardless of who composed it. Beyond the calculations, they liked the reading matter and the personality of the man behind it. The spirit of celebrity worship was not yet as great as it came to be in later centuries, but for the time he lived in, Benjamin Banneker had become a well-known figure.

The total circulation achieved is not known, but it was far enough into the thousands to be a solid commercial success. Most important of all was the satisfaction of those who had bought it, for that would indicate whether new editions could

Benjamin Banneker—although the name is misspelled, this is said to be the only portrait of him made from life. The present copy, taken from the Maryland Historical Society, has been clarified with a computer process devised by Dr. James G. Huckenpahler, making it perhaps the most accurate depiction of Banneker in existence. (Maryland Historical Society)

be assured of a profitable sale in the years to come. The letters that flowed in were enough to make that point clear. Each of the printers who had taken part in the distribution had profited handsomely. And, of course, Banneker had a solid financial return that made another old dream of his come true. He reduced the amount of acreage planted with commercial crops, may have hired a worker who would do most of the physical labor, and limited his own efforts to a kitchen garden, a few fruit trees, and the beekeeping that he regarded as a form of pleasurable study. His schedule was an inversion of the program he had been forced to keep during the Washington survey, and now it was for an enterprise of his own: studying the stars late into the night, sleeping very late in the morning, and then having ample time to meditate and to prepare his future editions without pressure or haste. The transition period of his life had passed; the tobacco farmer had become a writer.

But a few months before this publishing triumph, one highly significant reader had seen an advance copy of the almanac. Benjamin Banneker had taken great pains to write a special copy in his own hand, and he had sent it to Secretary of State Thomas Jefferson with what is surely one of the most explosive covering letters ever composed.

13

A Declaration
of Indignation

It was in August 1791, four months before his first almanac
would appear publicly, that Banneker sent the advance copy
to the second most important man in America. And the
accusatory anti-slavery letter that went with it should rank as a
pivotal document in the nation's history.

Three things made 1791 the defining year of Banneker's
life—the survey of Washington, the publication of his first
almanac, and his letter to Jefferson—and it is arguable that the
last was what made it truly an *annus mirabilis*, his miracle year.
Launching a verbal attack on the country's founders and putting himself in the potential line of fire from many vicious pro-
slavery adherents went against his inherited traits and his
upbringing. His Dogon ancestors and his own parents and
grandparents were stouthearted people whose disciplined courage told them to keep a low profile. Knowing how small they
were in numbers, how easily overpowered by the hordes around
them, they used their intelligence to survive, avoiding confrontation. That was not only Banneker's heritage; it was his

personality. For such a person to write to Jefferson as he did was like a deer turning to attack a lion. Astonishingly, this quiet-living man whom some have criticized for his long apparent indifference to social injustice suddenly challenged the system and its leaders with blazing words.

Banneker, who had once looked askance at abolitionist societies for fear they might cause him to be a target of white wrath, had undergone a hazardous change of heart. He had formerly questioned the wisdom of using a few individuals like himself as role models, fearing it would be misunderstood to imply that all blacks have equally fine minds. He knew that this process, called "synecdoche"—pretending that one person or event can typify a whole class—is irrational and can actually promote a form of racism. Now he had moved one hundred and eighty degrees to the conviction that publicizing his success might do more good than harm if it awakened the country to the senselessness of slavery. Even his premonition of physical danger was suppressed in a sudden determination to use his new stature as a surveyor and his almanac as platforms for declaring war on injustice.

The year 1791 was more than half a century before the words of black scholars and activists began to appear as a part of our national picture. Yet Banneker's sudden fiery reproach summarized everything that could have been said by an army of protesters. And it was all the more telling because it was virtually a personal attack on the man whose Declaration of Independence fifteen years earlier had set a world-acclaimed standard, asserting that the founders had failed to live by that standard and were making no visible effort to put it into practice.

Banneker's inactivity up to this point probably doesn't deserve either blame or praise. There was no precedent for a black person to become what would now be called an "activist," and it is understandable that a quiet person like Banneker had been reluctant to let white abolitionists use him as a role model for their cause, given the obvious potential dangers. But to go from that bland posture to the attack he made calls for a new assessment of Banneker's true nature.

It is clear that his career achievements were essentially his own, not the result of the Ellicotts' influence. He had shown genius long before their arrival, and their help was the kind of contribution that many persons, regardless of color, receive when fortunate contacts facilitate their advancement. There can be no question that Banneker had a great mind, independent of the Ellicotts. Now, the explosive turning point of 1791 may provide grounds for rethinking his inner strength. The decision to write Jefferson and the letter itself shed light on his true character.

Clearly, it was the change in his own circumstances that made Banneker take an action he had so firmly avoided before. It might have been expected that he would feel more cautious than ever, so as not to endanger the fruits of his accomplishments, and yet he took exactly the opposite course. Banneker grasped this success as the key to a stage door that must be opened, regardless of risk. For one thing, he suddenly had access to the men who had produced the play and were continuing to direct it badly. He now knew some of the leaders personally. If he mounted the stage, they would not wonder what obscure little farmer was making these sounds. They would know where the cries came from, recognize the name and the voice. Such an act might still prove self-destructive, but it would not necessarily be a wasted effort. In assessing his action, however, the question arises whether the astonishing thought of writing a rationally indignant letter to the Secretary of State occurred first to him, or whether the abolition-minded Ellicotts originated the idea. And once the thought had been mentioned, did the Ellicotts press their friend Benjamin to put his life and his newfound success on the line, or did he make the decision freely?

It is known that Banneker pondered long and hard before deciding to send the letter, but that would be no more than common sense. To compose and send it without a great deal of reflection would have been more foolish than heroic. History, however, has tended to hint that the Ellicotts were at his elbow, pressuring him to take the great leap. It was a dangerous decision for them, too, for their close ties to Banneker were so well known that many of the political leaders would think them responsible. But with their wealth and standing, they would be risking only unpopularity or loss of status, not life and limb. Banneker might have been risking everything. A black slave suspected of talking conspiratorially to a friend on a nearby plantation could be thrashed or have an ear cut off. What might be done to a black man who suggested a complete overthrow of the slave system—and put it in writing? Might some of Jefferson's great friends think up legal charges to bring against a black person who accused the nation's leaders of base behavior? If the letter was publicized, as it came to be, might he be charged with libel or blasphemy and fined enough to lose at least his property? No one could know, because no black person had ever tried such a thing. In an era when a black person was usually barred from even being a witness in a legal case involving a white person, how could an African American contemplate launching an accusation against the greatest white patriots? This level of daring towered above even the risks taken by later civil rights leaders.

There is no way to know who first uttered the idea aloud. It could certainly have been the creative George Ellicott, and one can hear him saying, "You know, Ben, now that Jefferson knows who you are, you should write to him, send him a copy of your ephemeris, and ask whether he still thinks that negroes are incapable of mental effort, as he wrote in that essay of his called

Notes on Virginia. Ask what he was thinking of when he said, 'All men are created equal.'"

But it is at least equally conceivable that Banneker, as he often did when he had an interesting idea, left a note at George's home, asking if he thought a copy of the almanac should be sent to Jefferson and wondering whether it seemed appropriate to include some sentences on the subject of slavery.

What is much more fathomable, however, is the nature of what transpired in the weeks between that original thought and the moment on August 19, 1791, when Banneker read his own carefully and beautifully handwritten words for one last time and consigned them to the mails. Some scholars have begun to back away from the historical supposition that the Ellicotts master-minded the letter, citing indications that Banneker showed a real wish to make his points. In fact, a careful look at the per-sonalities of the men involved, aided by some inductive reason-ing, can justify a much firmer position on this.

The nature, the organization, and the word choices of the letter itself proclaim it to be a Banneker product. Strangely enough, the more formally educated Ellicotts were not in Ban-neker's class as writers. George, brilliant and devoted to English literature as he was, wrote hasty letters with occasional mis-spellings and pedestrian words. Andrew, military man and mathe-matician, wrote straightforward facts with little sign of nuance. Even allowing for the likelihood that either man would have exerted his best powers in writing to the Secretary of State, their contributions would have been easily detectable in the pages signed by Banneker. Those pages are the work of a born writer, one with the same flair for pace, meter, and tone that Jefferson himself had.

The organization of the letter, the precise buildup and se-quence of the arguments, made it worthy of study by future generations—as other masterpieces of clear reasoning have been. Edmund Burke's two long addresses to Parliament in 1774 and 1775 in defense of the American colonists, for example, have been studied and even parsed by high school and college students because they were not just oratory, but surgically precise proofs that Britain was on the wrong side of history in thinking it could dominate these other Englishmen. And Burke demonstrated why nothing England might gain by war could match the rich revenues and power that she already enjoyed from these colonies. A similarly compelling logic and irresistible momentum are at work in Banneker's letter.

We are entitled to wonder whether these thoughts had been in Banneker's mind since the American Revolution ended with no sign that slavery would be abolished—or even since his earliest days, when he deplored the unjust treatment of Native Americans. What could such a bright mind have thought about his place in this society and the unspeakably worse place of the enslaved blacks? Some historians have pointed out that he was not confronted with day-to-day reminders of injustice. After all, the neighboring white farm families he had known all his life were mainly pleasant. Even the few nearby whites who owned two or three slaves are said to have been good bosses who treated these blacks much the same as other hired hands. Day-to-day reminders, perhaps not, but he must have noticed that they invited each other for social occasions without including their black neighbors. That was accepted as routine, never talked of as a slight, but it surely entered into people's minds and certainly into a mind as bright as Banneker's. It would be nonsense to think that racial inequality was not seared into his very rational brain as behavior that was utterly without a logical basis.

The precocious little Benjamin who, at age six, was advising neighbors of whatever race on how to balance their accounts would hardly have accepted any notion of inferiority. Nor would he have failed to notice that the white Quaker schoolmaster who befriended him had more knowledge than anyone he had known, yet took no notice of race. Benjamin also knew that his beloved grandmother, the redoubtable Big Ma-Ma, was a white who took great pride in her alliance with a black of noble heritage. The love and respect he had for her was one of the strongest ties in his early life—and her sense of status was based on character rather than color. The lesson didn't have to be told to him; it was there for him to see. It can be presumed that Banneker grew up with a remarkably evenhanded view of the world, judging persons mainly on the basis of how they judged others.

If so, it is more than likely that the young Benjamin had been silently disapproving of the skewed world he had been born into since his years as a precocious little boy. And the man who would grow from that child would never have accepted the failed promises of political leaders in the casual way that ordinary people do. Only when he was nearly middle age did the fresh words of the Declaration of Independence make him think briefly that a new and sane world was dawning at last. From the moment this one bright hope had begun to dim in 1781, the disgust expressed in his letter to Jefferson must have been fermenting in his mind. What was he to think now of the United States of America or of the leaders who spoke and wrote so finely while holding millions of innocents—even the newborn—in captivity? If he continued to think that the founding fathers were truly superior to the society around them, their failure would have seemed even worse, and he must have gone over and over in his mind the words "how pitiable it is . . . that you should at the same time be found guilty of that most criminal act," and perhaps dreamed of being able to say it to one of their number.

The thought of taking action against this bitter disappointment must have kept growing within him as the 1780s passed and hope dwindled. Banneker had seen that there were more cases of manumission, but the masters who freed slaves usually had an economic reason. The plantations that needed even more slaves were moving in the opposite direction. Private abolitionist groups were sincere, but quite small and lacking in clout. Governments, state and national, made few moves to heed them. Now he was actually acquainted with the man who was most responsible for those precious words "created equal." Whoever originated the idea of writing to Jefferson, Banneker must have considered it a great inspiration.

Even at that, it seems unlikely that he planned from the start to write a ringing protest. More plausibly, the sequence of events was much as he so candidly stated near the end of his letter. In his words, this "enlargement" of the letter "was not originally my design." That is, he first thought that just sending a copy of his almanac would be a good way to make his point. Thomas Jefferson had talked and written inconclusively about the mental abilities of the races. Here, at last, would be the resounding proof that a black—and one with almost no formal education—had actually mastered a subject that only a handful of scholarly whites could tackle. Sending this proof that the work was entirely his meant so much to him that he took the great trouble of handwriting the entire forty-eight-page publication rather than waiting to send the printed version. He then probably began to write a simple letter of transmission, but, although there is no way to prove this, his days of considering the project had made him more and more fearful that Jefferson would brush it off by having an aide send a simple letter of thanks. In that case, the whole opportunity would have been lost. The construction of the letter makes it likely that Banneker started writing additional paragraphs, trying to outline his plea for justice in a brief way, then adding more and more as it became apparent that there were so many arguments to be made. In the end, these pages could have seemed so powerful that he decided to reverse the order, making the letter the main communication, rather than simply a cover letter, and turning the almanac into Exhibit A.

There were at least two weeks of indecision—editing, re-writing, consulting with George Ellicott. There were certainly moments of doubt about the wisdom of the whole idea. Possibly Banneker held back and may have had to be reassured. But the historic chance to make a declaration such as no black man had ever made before, to send it to the most appropriate target of all, and to accompany it with a prepublication version of the greatest piece of anti-racist evidence ever produced up to that time—all these made it a virtual certainty that the letter was going to be sent, enthusiastically on Banneker's part. It read:

> Maryland, Baltimore County
> Near Ellicott's Lower Mills, August 19, 1791
> Thomas Jefferson, Secretary of State
>
> Sir, I am fully sensible of the greatness of that freedom which I take with you on the present occasion, a liberty which seemed to me scarcely allowable, when I reflected on that distinguished and dignified station in which you stand; and the almost general prejudice and prepossession which is so prevalent in the world against those of my complexion.
>
> I suppose it is a truth too well attested to you to need a proof here that we are a race of beings who have long labored under the abuse and censure of the world, that we have long been looked upon with an eye of contempt, and that we have long been considered rather as brutish than human, and scarcely capable of mental endowments.
>
> Sir, I hope I may safely admit, in consequence of that report which hath reached me, that you are a man far less

inflexible in sentiments of this nature than many others; that you are measurably friendly and well disposed towards us, and that you are willing and ready to lend your aid and assistance to our relief from those many distresses and numerous calamities to which we are reduced.

Now, Sir, if this is founded in truth, I apprehend you will readily embrace every opportunity to eradicate that train of absurd and false ideas and oppinions which so generally prevail with respect to us, and that your sentiments are concurrent with mine, which are that one universal Father hath given being to us all, and that he hath not only made us all of one flesh, but that he hath also without partiality afforded us all with the Same Sensations, and endued us all with the same faculties, and that however variable we may be in society or religion, however diversified in situation or color, we are all of the Same Family, and Stand in the Same relation to him.

Sir, if these are sentiments of which you are fully persuaded, I hope you cannot but acknowledge that it is the indispensable duty of those who maintain for themselves the rights of human nature, and who profess the obligations of Christianity, to extend their power and influence to the relief of every part of the human race from whatever burthen or oppression they may unjustly labour under, and this I apprehend a full conviction of the truth and obligation of these principles should lead all to.

Sir, I have long been convinced that if your love for yourSelves and for those inesteemable laws which preserve to you the rights of human nature, was founded on Sincerity, you could not but be solicitous that every Individual of whatsoever rank or distinction might with you equally enjoy the blessings thereof, neither could you rest satysfied, short of the most active diffusion of your exertions, in order to their promotion from any State of degradation, to which the unjustifyable cruelty and barbarism of men may have reduced them.

Sir, I freely and Cheerfully acknowledge, that I am of the African race, and, in that colour which is natural to them of the deepest dye*; and it is under a Sense of the most profound gratitude to the Supreme Ruler of the universe, that I now confess to you, that I am not under that State of tyrannical thralldom and inhuman captivity, to which too many of my brethren are doomed; but that I have abundantly tasted of the fruition of those blessings which proceed from that free and unequalled liberty with which you are favored and which I hope you will willingly allow you have received from the Hand of that Being from whom proceedeth every good and perfect gift.

Sir, suffer me to recall to your mind that time in which the arms and tyranny of the British Crown were exerted with every powerful effort, in order to reduce you to a State of Servitude; look back I intreat you on the variety of dangers to which you were exposed, reflecting on that time in which every human aid appeared unavailable, and in which even hope and fortitude wore the aspect of inability to the Conflict, and you cannot but be led to a Serious and grateful Sense of your miraculous and providential preservation. You cannot but acknowledge, that the present freedom and tranquillity which you enjoy you have mercifully received, and that it is the peculiar blessing of Heaven.

This, Sir, was a time in which you clearly saw into the injustice of a State of Slavery, and in which you had just apprehensions of the horrors of its condition, it was now, Sir, that your abhorrence thereof was so excited, that you publickly held forth this true and invaluable doctrine, which is worthy to be recorded and remembered in all succeeding ages. "We hold these truths to be self evident, that all men are created equal, and that they are endowed by their creator

---

* My father was brought here a Slave from Africa

with certain inalienable rights, that amongst these are life, liberty and the persuit of happiness."

Here, Sir, was a time in which your tender feelings for your selves engaged you thus to declare, you were then impressed with proper ideas of the great valuation of liberty, and the free possession of those blessings to which you were entitled by nature; but Sir how pitiable it is to reflect, that although you were so fully convinced of the benevolence of the Father of mankind, and of his equal and impartial distribution of those rights and privileges which he had conferred upon them, that you should at the same time counteract his mercies, in detaining by fraud and violence so numerous a part of my brethren under groaning captivity and cruel oppression, that you should at the same time be found guilty of that most criminal act, which you professedly detested in others, with respect to yourselves.

Sir, I suppose that your knowledge of the situation of my brethren is too extensive to need a recital here; neither shall I presume to prescribe methods by which they may be relieved, otherwise than by recommending to you, and all others, to wean yourselves from those narrow prejudices which you have imbibed with respect to them, and as Job proposed to his friends "Put your Souls in their Souls' stead," thus shall your hearts be enlarged with kindness and benevolence towards them, and thus shall you need neither the direction of myself or others in what manner to proceed herein.

And now, Sir, altho my sympathy and affection for my brethren hath caused my enlargement thus far, I ardently hope that your candour and generosity will plead with you in my behalf, when I make known to you, that it was not originally my design; but that having taken up my pen in order to direct to you as a present, a copy of an Almanack which I have calculated for the succeeding year, I was unexpectedly and unavoidably led thereto.

This calculation, Sir, is the production of my arduous study, in this my advanced stage of life; for having long had unbounded desires to become acquainted with the secrets of nature, I have had to gratify my curiosity herein thro my own assiduous application to Astronomical Study, in which I need not to recount to you the many difficulties and disadvantages which I have had to encounter.

And altho I had almost declined to make my calculation for the ensuing year, in consequence of that time which I had allotted therefor being taken up at the Federal Territory by the request of Mr. Andrew Ellicott, yet finding myself under several engagements to printers of this state to whom I had communicated my design, on my return to my place of residence, I industriously apply'd myself thereto, which I hope I have accomplished with correctness and accuracy, a copy of which I have taken the liberty to direct to you, and which I humbly request you will favourably receive, and altho you may have the opportunity of perusing it after its publication, yet I chose to send it to you in manuscript previous thereto, that thereby you might not only have an earlier inspection, but that you might also view it in my own hand writing.

And now Sir, I shall conclude and subscribe my self with the most profound respect,

Your most Obedient humble Servant
Benjamin Banneker

N.B. any communication to me may be had by a direction to Mr. Elias Ellicott merchant in Baltimore Town.

B.B.

Another postscript was added below, asking Jefferson to avoid having this manuscript published or giving it to any printer, since Banneker already had it in the hands of other printers. A telling touch, indeed. A few months earlier, he had been unable to find anyone willing to print his work. Now, far from needing any assistance from the great Jefferson in helping to publicize it, Banneker was letting him know that his earlier engagements had priority.

14

‿‿◞

A Founder's
Crafty Response

To his credit, Jefferson swallowed the rebuke and did nothing to punish the letter writer in return. Although Banneker suffered numerous threatening incidents in the remaining years of his life and a very destructive attack on his property after his death, they were very likely the work of racists or anti-abolitionists who wanted to stifle his potential as a role model for black liberation. There is no evidence whatsoever that they were inspired by Jefferson in any way.

The Secretary of State, who became a very successful two-term President some years later, received Banneker's letter on August 26 and sent an apparently appreciative reply within four days, reading as follows:

> Philadelphia, Aug. 30, 1791
>
> SIR, I thank you sincerely for your letter of the 19th instant and for the Almanac it contained. No body wishes more than I do to see such proofs as you exhibit, that nature has given to our black brethren, talents equal to the other colors of

men, and that the appearance of a want of them is owing merely to the degraded condition of their existence, both in Africa and America. I can add with truth, that nobody wishes more ardently to see a good system commenced for raising the condition of both their body and mind to what it ought to be, as fast as the imbecility of their present existence, and other circumstances which cannot be neglected, will admit.

I have taken the liberty of sending your Almanac to M. de Condorcet, Secretary of the Academy of Sciences at Paris, and member of the Philanthropic Society, because I considered it a document to which your color had a right for their justification against the doubts which have been entertained of them.

I am with great esteem, Sir, your most obedient humble servant.

Thomas Jefferson

Mr. Benjamin Banneker
Near Ellicott's Lower Mills, Baltimore Co.

Several mindless mistakes that have often been made about this correspondence and about Jefferson should be quickly brushed aside. For one thing, Banneker has been criticized for having signed his letter "Your most obedient humble servant." It will be noted that Jefferson responded in much the same way, for that was the common usage of the day. It had even less meaning than our use of "Yours sincerely," for we may sometimes feel sincerity, while no one in the eighteenth century was expressing the slightest sense of humility or servitude. Banneker was showing that he knew the gentlemanly style, and Jefferson was returning the courtesy, which some whites of that day would have refused to do.

Second, Jefferson has been excoriated by many for ever having questioned the equal intelligence of black persons and for having continued to own slaves until his death, despite his apparent relationship with Sally Hemings. He was certainly confused and conflicted on the subject, but the tendency to judge persons of earlier times as if they should have known what the future would teach is unfortunate. Only a very few persons of two centuries ago firmly believed that Africans had equal intellects, simply because blacks were seldom able to learn enough or do enough to overcome the hideous handicap they labored under. The few whites who saw through the curtain of obscurity should be honored as exceptionally thoughtful persons. But others—assuming that they were not cruel in their actions—should not be judged on that comparison. Jefferson's continued ownership of slaves was largely due to his dreadful failure in managing his property. He kept borrowing more and more money from banks because his absence from Monticello allowed the farm production to fall, and the times when he was at home brought far too many guests who wanted to stay with the great man. The bank loans he took out to cover the excessive expenses finally put him in such debt that it would have been impossible to free the slaves and provide them with enough money to ensure a good life. His best financial move would have been to sell the slaves, but that would have left them in slavery, and he genuinely seemed to fear that they would not be as well treated as they were at Monticello.

After giving him the benefit of the doubt, however, it must be said that Jefferson's ambivalent nature made it virtually certain that he would prove to be an unsatisfactory correspondent for Banneker. His duality on the subject was particularly marked, as shown repeatedly in his writings. The Jefferson Memorial in Washington, D.C., has an inscription about the immorality of slavery that sounds like the thinking of an enlightened modern person: "Can the liberties of a nation be secure when we have removed a conviction that these liberties are the gift of God? Indeed I tremble for my country when I reflect that God is just, that his justice cannot sleep forever. Commerce between master and slave is despotism. Nothing is more certainly written in the book of fate than that these people are to be free."

But while the chiseled words at the memorial end there, Jefferson's collected papers went on to say, "Nor is it less certain that the two races, equally free, cannot live in the same government. Native habit, opinion has drawn indelible lines of distinction between them." Not a vicious thought, perhaps, for blacks as well as whites have often felt that same way, even though they are being proved wrong. But Jefferson's apparently genuine belief that the two races represent totally different kinds of human beings made it impossible for him to see Banneker as a complete intellectual.

Even if the sincerity of this opinion is allowed, some very unfavorable traits in Jefferson were hidden in this apparently friendly reply to Banneker, as well as in subsequent events.

First, there is great duplicity in the wording of Jefferson's response to Banneker. The Secretary of State was a smooth writer, a nuanced writer, but here he was a slick writer. By pointedly mentioning the degraded condition of the blacks' existence "both in Africa and America" he makes it seem that they were as badly off before as they came to be in the slave system. Next, "the imbecility of their present existence" would appear to be a condemnation of the imbecilic *system*. But is it? It could also be taken to mean that for all he knew, perhaps most of the slaves themselves were imbeciles. Further on, "other circumstances which cannot be neglected" is surely a parenthetical reminder by Jefferson that the great financial investment in all the slaves was a quite natural barrier that made abolition a distant goal. And the overall impression is that Jefferson welcomes the almanac as one piece of affirmative evidence, but is definitely on the fence about whether there are enough intelligent black persons to bring about the improvements that he would wish to see. In other words, the short letter consists almost entirely of two-edged statements.

Jefferson was not at all wrong in thinking he needed to be very cautious with every word if he wished to go on with a political career. This reply, veiled as it is, caused him trouble years later when he was campaigning for the presidency. A column written by William Longton Smith was repeatedly quoted: "What shall we think of a Secretary of State thus fraternizing with negroes, writing them complimentary epistles . . . congratulating them on the evidence of their genius, and assuring them of his good wishes for their speedy emancipation?"

Not all his devious ways with this correspondence can be explained as mere political prudence. He did send the almanac to the Marquis de Condorcet, as he told Banneker. But his letter of transmittal showed him to be so eager to let his French friend see him as a champion of black advancement that he stooped to boasting of having personally arranged to use Banneker in the survey of Washington. His exact words were: "I procured him to be employed under one of our chief directors in laying out the new federal city on the Potowmac." The claim is a small point, a mere reminder that the author of one of the world's noblest documents could also descend to a petty untruth. Then he went on as if proclaiming Banneker's merits, telling Condorcet, "I have seen very elegant solutions of geometrical problems by him. Add to this that he is a very worthy and respectable member of society. I shall be delighted to see these instances of moral eminence so multiplied . . . "

Clearly, Jefferson was willing, even eager, to say things overseas that he would never say at home. Sadly, the marquis may never have seen the almanac, or if he did, there was probably no opportunity to make it better known in France, for it would have arrived just about the time that the continuing terror of the French Revolution caused him to be seized by the police. He died mysteriously in prison.

The petty boast to Condorcet would be minor if it did not contrast and conflict with another sequel that is seriously disillusioning. In a letter to a friend, Joel Barlow, Jefferson questioned whether Banneker could really have produced an almanac "without the suspicion of aid from Ellicott, his neighbor and friend." The slur was carelessly stated and totally without foundation. Andrew Ellicott, who had done his own calculations of this sort, was not a neighbor and had been no help at all to Banneker with his almanac. George Ellicott, the actual "neighbor and friend" of Banneker, had no experience of this kind. Worst of all, Jefferson went on to tell Barlow, "I have a long letter from Banneker, which shows him to have had a mind of very common stature indeed."

That remark, even if we generously assume that Jefferson knew nothing of Banneker's lack of formal education, is shocking when applied to a person of supposedly inferior race who had raised himself to a professional level as a mathematician-astronomer-watchmaker-surveyor. His literary style might not have pleased Jefferson, but any fair observer would declare it to be elegant, and his almanacs would soon be appealing to readers in a way comparable to the famed *Poor Richard's Almanac* that had won acclaim for the peerless Benjamin Franklin. Considering how Jefferson had praised Banneker in the letter to Condorcet, this statement of disdain is all the more inexcusable.

Scholars and biographers have not previously called Jefferson to account for the clear falsehood he committed in this disparity between his two opposing statements. Nor have they pondered what could have caused his great mind to plunge to such a foolish and mean-spirited misjudgment. Two possibilities occur; some have suspected that Sally Hemings was unfaithful to Jefferson, perhaps with a younger member of his family, and this might conceivably have soured the Secretary of State's thoughts on race. But the underlying premise is weak, for it is said that Hemings faithfully brought flowers to Jefferson's grave for the rest of her life. The more obvious possibility is that Banneker's indignant letter to Jefferson, so determinedly skewering him for continuing to keep slaves in total disregard of his own fine words, had infuriated him far more than he let on.

In that sense, Banneker's letter had one flaw. If he really had hoped to turn Jefferson's thoughts in his favor, its accusatory tone had doomed it to failure. A plea to a one-man jury has no chance if it accuses that person of being a party to "guilt," "fraud," and "criminal acts." The words were justified, but hurling them at a lone juror was bound to fail, unless that man were a saint. Jefferson, of course, should have seen that Banneker's points were exactly right, but not for the first time, a great mind preferred to despise the attacker rather than admit its own error.

On the other hand, Banneker's letter was perfectly crafted for the great public jury that would later read it. When the first almanac was about to be printed, Banneker's supporters and the printers urgently discussed whether to include the correspondence. It was left out of the first run, but both Banneker's letter and Jefferson's reply were included in some later printings. And the exchange was quoted many times over the next half-century as the argument over abolition heated up.

Perhaps neither Jefferson nor the entire leadership of the United States could have done much to meet Banneker's demands, regardless of their inclinations; to have challenged the institution of slavery would have split the new country, leaving one free nation in the North and a slave nation in the South. No one can say for certain what would have resulted if the great minds that had united to create the United States of America had concentrated their mental, financial, and strategic firepower as determinedly on liberty for all as they had once concentrated on freedom from England. Or, alternatively, they might have refrained from an immediate challenge to the Southern states on this issue, but made it absolutely clear that they despised slavery and would not go on for long with the growing addiction to it. They could have presented proposals for a step-by-step process to reduce the reliance on slave labor and make provisions for the education and training that would have turned the freed persons into citizens.

There were people who said these things all along, people who worked and took risks in the furtherance of such ideas. There were even Americans who, sometimes with good motives, contributed large sums of money to impractical and wrong-headed schemes for repatriating slaves to Africa. The problem was that there were far too few persons who felt any responsibility at all on the subject. And hardly any of the men who had been willing to fight in the cause of national freedom now wanted any part of the risks involved in making personal freedom a goal. The same persons who had been daring young men with a sense of mission had become cautious older men with a love of prudence. Tom Paine, whose fighting words had kept the Revolution alive in its darkest days, was now shunned as a troublemaker by the leadership. Hardly any of his old comrades wanted to be seen talking to him. In this young nation with an already graying government, to have spoken for Banneker would have been politically incorrect.

15

A Place Among
the Greats

A single thought that he expressed in less than a hundred words, and at least a century and a half before modern telescopes could confirm it, should place Banneker among the immortals of astronomy. Other scientists have said they had only one real idea in their entire lives, a lightning flash—a totally new thought that was a leap from accumulated findings of the past. In Banneker's case, this was an inspiration that took his mind far beyond the solar system to theorize very positively that each of the stars was a central sun and that many of them had planets circling them. This idea appeared in print in his almanac of 1792, which he actually worked on in 1790. It was worded as such an established fact that it seems likely to have come to him much earlier, perhaps in the 1750s, when time and space held a major place in his thoughts.

Almost as astonishing as the concept itself is the fact that it has been reprinted a number of times, but simply accepted as one more interesting point, never singled out as the historic event it was. The entire essay is reprinted near the end of this book, but the key lines should be noted here:

> This sun, with all its attendant planets, is but a very little part of the grand machine of the universe; every star, though in appearance no bigger than the diamond that glitters upon a lady's ring, is really a vast globe, like the sun in size and glory; no less spacious, no less luminous, than the radiant source of the day: So that every star is not barely a world, but the centre of a magnificent system; has a retinue of worlds, irradiated by its beams, and revolving round its attractive influence, all of which are lost to our sight in unmeasurable wilds of ether.

Here Banneker was expressing almost matter-of-factly (and in words that are nearly accurate to this day) the existence of extra-solar planets, a concept that only a few scientists would touch on in the century after his death and that astronomy would turn to with fascination only in the twentieth century. Banneker did not "discover" these planets, which remain invisible, but are now provable by several other means. Banneker's insight was an intuition that was bolstered by his observation that every design and pattern found in nature tends to be repeated throughout the known universe. He felt, therefore, that it was unthinkable for the creative force to have made one successful solar system and none other like it.

Two other thinkers are known to have mentioned such a possibility before: Thomas Wright, an Englishman who was not widely read or influential, suggested in a 1750 volume, *A New Hypothesis of the Universe*, that the nebulae are really galaxies and that our solar system is only one of many galactic structures, implying that there could be many "suns" with unseen planets. And much earlier, in the sixteenth century, the monk Giordano Bruno was killed by the Inquisition for having challenged church teaching by voicing a similar theory. There is no evidence that Banneker ever knew of either thinker, but the possibility has to be taken into account. Even if he had somehow read about such a hypothesis or heard of it from his friend George Ellicott, Banneker's feat in grasping this as a defining principle of the cosmos and expanding on it as he did would have been remarkable. Just as modern research often leads to parallel scientific discoveries in a number of countries—and all sometimes become Nobel laureates—the least that could be said of Banneker would be that he was apparently one of only three persons who had expounded such a theory up to that time, a great feat even for a professional astronomer with a distinguished résumé.

It would also be reasonable, however, to go beyond that and say that Banneker actually stood alone, as he was the only one whose theory was based on reason, on an examination of facts, rather than faith. Both Bruno and Wright cited faith-based convictions for their insistence that multiple worlds exist. Giordano Bruno, seeing things more as a monk than as an astronomer, said there must be an infinite number of worlds because God is within and through all things, which led some observers to call his system pantheistic. Thomas Wright was a clockmaker by trade, whose speculation that the Deity could be found in the center of the universe led him to conclude that the nebulae are other "abodes of the blessed."

Partly because these hypotheses seemed to be more religion than logic, the science of astronomy had failed to react to them. No leading astronomer up to Banneker's day—neither Copernicus, nor Galileo, nor any major scholar—had expressed definitive thoughts on what lay beyond our solar system. They knew that the stars must be distant bodies, but not at all that they replicated the relationship of our sun and its planets. For one thing, they were misled by the fact that the most powerful telescopes showed no sign of planets beyond our own system; they failed to reckon with the possibility that dark objects might simply be invisible from many light-years away. Even among the few who took any interest in extra-solar planets before the twentieth century, hardly any thought it worthwhile to consider the chance that they might contain life. Since the planets in our solar system clearly become less and less habitable as their distance from the sun increases, they reasoned that surely nothing even farther from the sun could harbor life, ignoring the fact that those more distant planets might have suns of their own, as Banneker asserted so positively. Banneker alone, although he had a strong faith in the existence of a Creator, was thinking as a modern scientist does—preferring to experiment with tangibles whenever possible or at least to reason on the basis of observations, wherever that reasoning might lead.

Banneker not only fixed on this new thought, but he went a giant step farther and anticipated the twentieth-century belief that some of those myriad planets must, as a matter of statistical probability, be capable of supporting life. As he looked at stars in the night sky, he even imagined that an intelligent being on one such extra-solar planet was looking back at him, seeing our sun as just one of the bright specks in his sky, and, just as naively as a watcher on Earth, continuing to suppose that the whole cosmos had been created solely to make his own planet the only home of thoughtful life. Banneker was saying—as no one said with such an air of certitude until the era of the Hubbell telescope was almost at hand—that this is probably the universe full of communities and beings, prevented by distance from imagining how much company they have, much as a tribe of early cave dwellers might have thought itself alone before venturing to explore the terrifying wilderness that separated it from other such communities.

Not even the leading scientists of Banneker's own day, closer to our time than to Galileo's, with the finest equipment known, had yet come to this idea. And it is puzzling that no review of Banneker's writings has noted how high a place he deserves in the history of astronomy. Compared to this, nothing else in his life can compete in importance. There would be practical accomplishments that the world of affairs and commerce might hold in higher esteem, but they would be measuring by an inferior yardstick. Banneker's mental excursion outside our solar system declares that the simple tobacco farmer should long since have been singled out by the encyclopedias of astronomy. Note the following great names that have been recorded on this subject— and how far behind Benjamin Banneker they have all been:

In 1761, Johann Heinrich Lambert speculated, as Thomas Wright had, that groups of stars like our sun made up the Milky Way, but offered no thought that those stars might have planets around them. Two full generations later, Sir William Herschel worked on Lambert's idea. He was a German-born musician and scientist who became such a favorite in English society that he anglicized his name from "Wilhelm" and was knighted for several scientific findings, including the discovery of the planet Uranus. Because his sister Caroline was a great lens grinder, the brother–sister team could see far more in space than anyone else, and in 1823, seventeen years after Banneker's death, Herschel was able to confirm visual evidence that the stars are indeed like suns, and he told the Royal Society in a lecture that they might also have planetary systems. This was the first modern step in the direction of Banneker's eighteenth-century assertion. But it was more than a century after that, in 1943, before the Dutch American Peter van de Kamp, working at Swarthmore College, was able to prove that some stars are accompanied by planets. Because these planets were and remain invisible from Earth, since they are not luminous, their existence had to be proved by measuring how their central star wobbles due to their gravitational effect. This positive confirmation of planets outside our solar system was considered mind-boggling and finally led German scientists to theorize more emphatically that some of those planets might well be inhabited.

On this subject of extraterrestrial life, Banneker's intuition was one and a half to two centuries ahead of the scientists with fine educations, equipment, and opportunity for collegial discussion. If his station in life had given his thoughts a place in the scientific journals, the world might have taken these revolutionary ideas into account a century and a half earlier. The practical value of this can be disputed, since theories cannot be put to work if they come long before there is technology to test them. But as another indicator of mental ability, Banneker's lead is compelling.

The last few decades have brought leaps in astronomy that make one forget how modest the ideas about life on other planets were until quite recently. In the mid-nineteenth century, a renowned mathematician named Carl Friedrich Gauss was considered very avant-garde for ruminating about the possibility of life on the moon, but nothing beyond that. Then came speculation about the possible habitation of our neighbor planets, especially Mars. But since it was known that Jupiter, Saturn, Neptune, and Uranus were definitely uninhabitable, it was assumed that objects much farther away had to be ruled out entirely. The notion of making a mental leap to far more distant planets did not come into the picture.

How Banneker's mind could have made that leap with such assurance, even if it had been triggered by someone else's comment, is unknowable. Why did he ignore the daunting evidence of our own outer planets, lock on the more distant idea, and develop it as he did? It is important to realize that he was not casting about for novel ideas as a science fiction writer might have done. His words about the mutual looks between an earth-ling and the resident of some extra-solar planet were more than mere daydreaming. He was calculating what the patterns of nearby celestial objects might tell about the structure of outer space, assessing all the lessons of nearby astronomy before reasoning that the pattern of movement obeyed by Earth and its neighbor planets must be replicated in the far reaches of the cosmos. Those distant suns must be circled by planets. By that same comparative logic, he concluded that the laws of probability make it likely that some of those planets are the homes of beings who look toward us as sightlessly, yet wonderingly, as we look toward them. The thought was as stupefying in the 1700s as it is intriguing today.

The reason for Banneker's self-assurance on this point was probably his love of Creation's design and order. However and whenever the idea occurred to him, it must have immediately seemed to make good sense and caused the seed to take root. The perfect grace of objects circling a nucleus seemed too great an invention to be tried once and discarded. Using this pattern to make many duplicate solar systems fitted his concept of a natural order. If it appeared to diminish Earth's position in the scale of things, it would not have disturbed Banneker in the least. He knew all about lessons in humility and the counter-vailing thought that the humblest shall be exalted.

❧

Banneker must have had many other fascinating things to say about the cosmos in the early journals that went up in smoke when he died. For the occasional nugget, there are only later chance remarks that recall thoughts from his youth or the memoirs of other persons. A leading example relates accounts of his interest in a star named Sirius, also called the Dog Star because it is in the constellation sometimes called Canus Major. It is not surprising that Banneker took notice of it, for Sirius is one of the brightest stars in the night sky, but it is noteworthy that he felt a special affinity for this mysterious star, probably without knowing that it had fascinated the ancients of many lands. It was called Al-Ghul by Arab astronomers, because its name in Arabic means "ghoul," and its occasional shadowy look gives it a ghostly quality. What had long captivated astronomers was its changeable appearance—often called a "wavy" look, sometimes bright, but occasionally dull and clouded. This seemed to defy Aristotle's dictum that heavenly bodies are changeless. Today it is known that Sirius is, in fact, two stars, each with a different brightness, that circle around each other. These "disk-stars" have become even more interesting to astronomers as powerful telescopes make them more discernible.

But the fact that Banneker believed Sirius was actually two stars—before the world of astronomy knew this to be so—is eerily important because in this case, he may have had help, not from the scientific world, but from his African ancestors. In that case, it gives further confirmation of Banneker's Dogon heritage, for these people are said to have learned of the star's double life in some mysterious way centuries before. Banneker seems to have had his special interest in Sirius long before the brilliant English astronomer John Goodriche, a sickly deaf-mute who died at age twenty-two, would be the first person in the Western world to suggest the two-star theory in 1782, at the age of eighteen. It was 1890 before Hermann Vogel proved Goodriche right by showing how an invisible companion star circles around the main star and sometimes eclipses Al-Ghul's brightness. Banneker never had any equipment that could have discovered this. Some think he may have been drawn to Sirius because it represented the mood swings that he knew himself to have, despite his studied attempt to appear always placid and consistent. But what first called his attention to it? Some hint of this from Grandfather Banneka to Molly and from her to Benjamin seems a likelier explanation than any other. But that only increases the mystery, for there is no known explanation of how the Dogon people could have learned the star's secret without telescopes (see appendix I).

16

The Sage's Years of Glory

I t was not at all in Banneker's makeup to exult or gloat about the success of his almanac, but he did take a genuine pride in his triumph. Even before the publication was arranged, when he was being turned down by the printers, he was almost in awe of what he had accomplished in calculating a twelve-month ephemeris that he knew to be accurate. All his life, he had been as devoid of false modesty as he was of hubris or puffery. As a child who helped neighbors to straighten out their finances, he had recognized that he had an unusual mind. When he learned to handle scientific instruments that baffled highly educated persons, he was genuinely grateful to his Maker for the gifts he had been born with. But the feat of completing calculations that only the finest astronomers and mathematicians even attempted actually astonished him. Whether they were published or not, he felt that nothing could take away that satisfaction.

One additional bit of probable delight he never made mention of was a victory over Major Andrew Ellicott, his boss on the great survey project and a professional of such stature that he later became Professor of Mathematics at West Point Military Academy. Ellicott had calculated and written almanacs of his own, and they were solid successes, but "Ben's" consistently outsold his former superior's less lively product. While Banneker's gratitude to the Ellicotts for all their favors would have made him wish the major the best of luck with his competing almanac, coming out on top in this friendly rivalry could not have failed to be a great feeling.

The printers of the almanacs soon saw that they had been right to make a merit of the writer's race and of their wish to show the mental qualities that blacks were capable of. The first edition included this message:

> The Editors of the PENNSYLVANIA, DELAWARE, MARYLAND, and VIRGINIA Almanacks feel themselves gratified in the opportunity of presenting to the Public, through the medium of the Press, what must be considered an extraordinary effort of Genius—a COMPLETE and ACCURATE EPHEMERIS for the year 1792, calculated by a sable Descendant of Africa who, by this specimen of ingenuity, evinces to Demonstration that mental Powers and Endowments are not the exclusive Excellence of White People, but that the Rays of Science may alike illumine the Minds of Men of every Clime . . .

The favorable comments from readers grew to a very respectable number, large enough to show how many people were ready to accept this kind of precedent-shattering initiative. The one most noticed and quoted came from Maryland Senator James McHenry, a distinguished person who had been in the federal government and even in a presidential cabinet. He wrote an introduction to the 1792 almanac, which was also reprinted in several newspapers, flatly eliminating any suspicion

Portrait of Senator James McHenry. (Library of Congress collection)

that the work was not Banneker's or that it had been done with great help from others. The senator said, in part:

> I have been the more careful to investigate these particulars and to ascertain their reality, as they form an interesting fact in the history of man . . .
>
> I consider this Negro as fresh proof that the powers of the mind are disconnected with the colour of the skin . . . Let the issue be what it will, I cannot but wish on this occasion, to see the Public patronage keep pace with my black friend's merit.

The senator's hopes were amply met. Not only did the public buy the almanac actively, but very soon Banneker began to experience one of the happy burdens that popularity entails. The considerable number of letters from readers and his courteous attempts to answer them personally took much of the free time that he had expected to hoard for his own meditations. And he was stunned when visitors began appearing at his cabin door, wanting to see "the black sage in his own surroundings," as one visitor put it. He was sufficiently pleased by the compliment to enjoy the experience. And he seldom failed to ask a visitor to come in and stay for a bit. But being a rather enthusiastic conversationalist himself, he often allowed the talks to run on more than he expected. As the years of successful new editions continued, readers who had begun to feel like friends even at a distance were more and more likely to show up whenever they were in the Patapsco area. Banneker finally disciplined himself to tell any new arrival at the start that he had only a few minutes to spare. But it pained him to do that, for he had lived a rather lonely life, and the coming of an admirer who usually wanted to express agreement with the advice and philosophy in the Banneker almanac brought far more joy than aggravation.

Long-term weather forecasts were, of course, part of every almanac, and American astronomers had introduced slightly more conscientious methods than the English, who often used ludicrous exaggerations. There was an art to making most prognostications deliberately vague, using words like "variable winds" and "periods of unseasonable warmth." Banneker did his share of this, but he made a genuine attempt to include some of the proven wisdom he had learned from his African father and grandfather, along with observations of his own. One thing he explored carefully was the theory that phases of the moon might have an effect on weather in various localities, but this proved to have no merit. On the whole, his forecasts, which differed greatly from those of Andrew Ellicott, were some of the better attempts in this chaotic field. Also, Banneker's tide tables for the Chesapeake Bay area were considered by pilots and fishermen to be unusually fine and very useful.

Just as modern magazines often appear in separate regional versions, the Banneker almanac came to have separate editions for Baltimore, the Wilmington-Philadelphia area, and Virginia. This was done, in part, because it enabled some of the statistical data—such as tides and coastal conditions—to be customized for each area. But it was also because writers customarily made separate deals with printers in different cities, rather than giving one printer rights for all the states. As a result, at least twenty-eight separate editions are known to have been published over a seven-year period. Most of these varied from thirty-two to forty-eight pages in length.

The successive editions also had variations in their covers and opening words, in their essays, and, of course, in their computations. Because he had always been inclined to consider how the world worked and think of ways to improve it, Banneker was amazed to realize how easily his once solitary thoughts were now reaching thousands of people. He privately thought it rather amusing that he had become a celebrity after six decades of living unknown—and he actively enjoyed it.

He even ventured into poetry, usually on a theme that coupled his wonder at the majesty of the universe and the naturally pious feelings that this evoked in him. The 1794 almanac, for example, contained these lines:

View yon majestic concave of the sky!
Contemplate well those glorious orbs on high—
These constellations shine, and comets blaze;
Each glitt'ring world the Godhead's pow'r displays!

Banneker's verses are like the solidly good efforts that might come from the pen of a highly educated gentleman of his time whose talent did not rise to that of a great natural poet. His obedience to meter, which was then much more of a requirement than it is now, has his usual precision. Especially noteworthy, however, is that his poetry shows the same talent for word choice that has previously been noted in his best prose writing. For instance, in the above lines, his use of the word "concave" as a noun—although most persons know it only as an adjective—is an unusual touch. As a rule, persons of average language ability know only one use for each word, and only the highly educated enrich their vocabularies by finding uncommon ways to use a common word.

Each year, he imagined he had included all he had to say. "Maybe there will be nothing to use next year," he once jotted in his journal. But invariably, all he had to do was sit quietly and consult his encyclopedic memory for new material, recalling his own thoughts or the family talk he had heard, especially from his talented mother, and he would come up with many more recipes, cures, helpful hints, and paragraphs of elevated wisdom before the next edition went to bed. The printer's cover would again justifiably describe him as "An American Sage" and promise "Several Useful Tables and Valuable Recipes" or "A Variety of Instructive and Entertaining Matter in Prose and Verse."

Some of the essays were printed with quotation marks enclosing the paragraphs, which has led to speculation that they were simply copied from some unnamed source. This is unlikely, because Banneker would not have been at all reluctant to mention important sources for his material. In one sense, given his limited access to research facilities, he probably would have felt that citing other prominent thinkers was a greater cause for pride than making his own arguments. Because most of the ideas in these quotation-marked passages reflect thoughts that Banneker had recorded in his journal at various times, it seems likely that he used the quotation marks in a different way from our modern usage—perhaps as an indication that the material included thoughts culled from a variety of sources.

In one sense, his vignettes of wit and wisdom could be considered a more notable accomplishment than the scientific calculations. That he was a mathematical wizard was a gift of nature. But the fact that what he had to say on so many subjects and the way he phrased it appealed to thousands of mostly white readers should have been an even greater proof of how much blacks and whites had in common—how much they could commune and converse if only they would try. This was the unspoken subject that was confirmed by so many of the visitors who sought him out. It was the unexpected range of his interests that made so many refer to him as a sage. They found that his concerns and his advice were very relevant to their own lives. What they had gleaned from his almanac they saw verified in person—that they were one people when they left their fear at the door.

Among the many letters Banneker received, a few were rude, questioning how much of the publication was his own and how much help from whites had been needed to create his almanac. But on the other hand, virtually all the visitors were abolitionists, who came hoping to find a man who validated their convictions. If there were any who came with a negative turn of mind, Banneker gave no sign of suspecting any such thing, and his manner and surroundings must have disarmed them. Not one person ever went off to write an unfavorable comment. His cabin was small and rustic, but the evidence of scholarship was on his large table and in every corner. Often, he moved to bring refreshments, and he talked in an engaging, unhurried way. A few of the visitors felt as if they had become friends, and began a correspondence with him as soon as they returned home. One of these, Susanna Mason, was among the persons referred to earlier who attested to having seen his wooden clock. Although her importance is more as a witness than as a poet, the lines she addressed to Banneker after a repeat visit in 1796 give an indication of the adulation—and perhaps unwanted advice—that he grew accustomed to receiving:

> An African astronomer.
> Thou need'st to have a special care,
> Thy conduct with thy talent square,
> That no contaminating vice,
> Obscure thy lustre in our eyes,
> Or cast a shade upon they merit,
> Or blast the praise thou might'st inherit;
> For folly in an orb so bright,
> Will strike on each beholder's sight;
> Nay, stand exposed from age to age,
> Extant on some historian's page,
> Now as thy welfare I intend,
> Observe my counsel as a friend.
> Let fair example mark thy round
> Unto thine orbit's utmost bound.
> "The good man's path," the scriptures say,
> "Shines more and more to perfect day."

Could all the strictures about his "conduct" possibly have meant that Mrs. Mason's visit happened to come at a time when Banneker had sipped too much wine? Some of the words are so strong—talk of "contaminating vice" that might "cast a shade" upon his merit—that they invite concern about some serious trait of Banneker's that has been overlooked. The few comments from others who knew Mrs. Mason make her sound like a well-meaning prude, and she may have enjoyed giving out finger-wagging strictures as a precaution against vices that had not really surfaced. It will be noted that the sentiments are arranged much like the progression often found in a sermon, with warnings against the prevalence of sin phasing into a triumphal ending. Whatever the explanation, it didn't blight the relationship, for she continued to correspond with Banneker enthusiastically.

After the success of the 1792 Banneker almanac, the printers took it for granted that this was to be a yearly staple. It did continue for five more lucrative years, 1793 through 1797. The preparation and printing of the almanacs went smoothly for the most part, although there was considerable discussion and decision-making on one questionable item in the second almanac, which went on sale in 1792 for the year 1793. The issue, as mentioned briefly earlier, was whether to include Banneker's correspondence with Jefferson. Banneker himself felt particularly conflicted about it, knowing as he did that the powerful words could have a great effect, yet wondering about the propriety of publicizing private letters. Also, it is a tremendous testimony to this man's capacity for honest self-examination and perfectionism that he was rather dissatisfied with his own letter whenever he reread it. He felt that it sounded stultified and pompous. And with an astonishing capacity for empathic thought, he often wondered what Jefferson felt on first reading his words. In the end, his hope of influencing other minds in the right direction won out, and he authorized Pemberton and Goddard & Angell to include the two letters in the next almanac.

Banneker now repeatedly returned to the injustice of slavery as one of his themes in the almanacs and in his personal writing. He knew that he was putting his life in danger with every one of these essays, and he recorded several more frightening incidents in his journal. But every such scare, which he did not take at all lightly, only gave him proof that his words were having an effect. Now that he had a platform from which to make himself heard, he raised his voice repeatedly. Sometimes this was done in highly competent, if not the most musical, verse. One more example of such an effort, written in late 1791 and then used in an almanac, reads this way:

> Behold ye Christians! and in pity see
> Those Afric sons which Nature formed free.
> Behold them in a fruitful country blest.
> Of Nature's bounties see them rich possest.
> Behold them herefrom torn by cruel force,
> And doomed to slavery without remorse.
> This act, America, thy sons have known
> This cruel act, relentless they have done.

Equally consistent was his unique way of combining scientific observations, put into simplified words that all could understand, with moral precepts. In these passages, he showed his own deep faith—his certainty that a single great Creator had carefully prepared a wonderful system for our comfort and had also set out clear guidelines for us to live by. This was exemplified by one essay called "Remarks on the Swiftness of Time." It began this way:

> The natural advantages which arise from the position of the earth we inhabit, with respect to the other planets, afford much employment to mathematical speculation, by which it has been discovered that no other conformation of the system could have given such commodious distributions of light and heat, or imparted fertility and pleasure to so great a part of the revolving sphere.
>
> It may be perhaps observed by the moralist, with equal reason, that our globe seems particularly fitted for the residence of a being, placed here for only a short time, whose

task is to advance himself to a higher and happier state of existence by unremitted vigilance of caution and activity of virtue . . .

To this end all the appearances of nature uniformly conspire. Whatever we see on every side, reminds us of the lapse of time and the flux of life. The day and the night succeed each other, the rotation of seasons diversifies the year, the sun rises, attains the meridian, declines and sets; and the moon every night changes its form. . . .

He that is carried forward, however swiftly, by a motion equable and easy, perceives not the change of place but by the variation of objects. If the wheel of life, which rolls thus silently along, passed on through undistinguishable uniformity, we should never mark its approaches to the end of the course . . . If the parts of life were not variously coloured, we should never discern their departure or succession, but should live thoughtless of the past and careless of the future, without will, and perhaps without power, to compute the periods of life, or to compare the time which is already lost with that which may probably remain . . .

Because he was such a dedicated pacifist, Banneker devoted several pages of the 1793 almanac to an essay on pacifism. He might very well have written on this subject himself, considering the strong Quaker influences in his life. But its poor quality shows that a guest writer must have been at work, and it is usually said to have been written by Benjamin Rush, a Philadelphia doctor and anti-slavery advocate. This is questionable because Rush was highly regarded by some of the wisest Founding Fathers, including the tough-minded John Adams. Because this was only Banneker's second almanac, and the joy of being able to put his own ideas into writing was one of the glories of this new field, it must have been an enormous sacrifice to let anyone else play so great a role in it. In any case, the words were so naively impractical that Banneker was fortunate his almanac did not lose readers because of this poor piece. The article was titled "A Plan for a Peace Office for the United States." The rather sophomoric approach was signaled when it began, "It is to be hoped that no objection will be made to the establishment of such an office while we are engaged in a war with the Indians, for as the War Office of the United States was established in time of peace, it is equally reasonable that a Peace Office should be established in time of war."

It then proceeded to outline how a Secretary of Peace would establish and maintain free schools in every city in the United States and would be responsible for finding schoolmasters who would instruct the youth of the country in reading, writing, and arithmetic, and in the doctrines of some religion, preferably Christianity. Considering the fact that the states had just barely been convinced to join a loose-knit union that left their states' rights intact, the nonsense of thrusting a federal school system on them (which the federal government would not dare to try even today) is clear. And to ignore the fact that separation of church and state was another dominant principle made this a piece of sheer nonsense. The article went on to stipulate that "militia laws should everywhere be repealed and military dress and titles be laid aside," and ended by suggesting the kinds of pictures to be shown on the walls of schools, including: "A group of French and Austrian soldiers dancing arm in arm" and "A lion eating straw with an ox and an adder playing upon the lips of a child." But the result of all this excess is that readers may have regarded it as an intentional bit of comedy, for when the following year's almanac came out, the sales were even greater.

Whatever the true cause, 1794 proved to be the peak of Banneker's almanac career, with the highest sales he had ever known. The number of regular buyers had built up considerably, and it was also a time when abolitionism was at a high point, making a dual reason for buying this particular almanac. This success even brought on the idea of selling the publication in England, and Banneker went to the trouble of preparing an ephemeris for the purpose. Even though the anti-slavery activists in England were keen on everything dealing with Banneker and passages from his works were read in the House of Commons, the financial arrangements were never worked out, and the almanac was not published abroad.

After 1794, although there would be three more reasonably profitable years for the regular American editions, the liveliest sales were past. More competitors had entered the field, for one thing, but, also, the abolitionist societies proved, sadly, to have been more of a fad than a crusade. Some actually went out of existence, and nearly all saw waning interest. The extra sales that had resulted from that source of enthusiasm were lost.

Banneker was not unduly distressed by his decision to retire from the almanac market. His health was declining, and the chore of preparing more editions was a tiring one. After the last edition, of 1797, was published, he continued to calculate the ephemeris year after year, well into the nineteenth century, but only as a mental exercise for his own satisfaction.

17

Living Off the Land Again

The early 1800s saw Benjamin Banneker's talent for ingenuity, arithmetical skill, and prudent management in full flower. Now in his early seventies (which was then considered a great age), he was surprisingly inventive in working out ways to make his late years into good ones.

With the revenues from the almanacs at an end, he needed to create a regular income in order to go on living comfortably. What he thought of, a little guiltily, as extravagances were almost pitifully small items—a few food specialties, tobacco for his pipe, a little wine or brandy to lend life to very simple mealtimes, an occasional pair of new shoes, and, above all, reading matter. Along with books to feed his insatiable mind, he now regularly scoured the local newspaper to search for signs of the path his state and country were taking. Such lavish living would be impossible without somehow earning eight to ten dollars per month. His only asset was his land, most of which was now lying unused. Going back to the uncertain rewards of active farming—even with the help of hired hands—would have taken too much time away from the pleasure of contemplation. He decided to use his land in another way. His first thought was to rent parcels of it to neighbors, and he actually made several such deals, but fortunately on a short-term trial basis, for this proved to be a disaster.

It soon became clear that being a landlord was not at all suited to his temperament, for he found that it involved the irritating task of trying to collect rents. He had thought of the arrangement as if his tenants were much like himself, punctual in meeting their obligations and therefore a steady source of income. Instead, they proved unreliable and even prone to show resentment toward a person who expected cash in return for unused acres. Rent collection dates became very painful. Within a year, he had heard most of the excuses that any experienced landlord would recognize—the crop that failed, the impossible weather, the pests that had taken control, the family illnesses, all delivered with shifty looks or sullen stares. The old neighborly feeling suffered in the process. Indeed, he even had to wonder whether some of the quasi-terrorist threats that he recounted in his journal could have been mounted by angry tenants rather than racist rogues. "Better to die of hunger than of anger," Banneker concluded in one of his journal entries, and he gave up on the rental scheme.

He turned, instead, to an ingenious form of annuity, based on a deferred sale of land to the Ellicotts. He calculated that about three-fourths of his land was worth $1180. Next, he considered the rather short lifetimes of his father and grandfather, and he estimated that he would certainly not live more than another decade. He proposed that the Ellicotts agree to pay him $112 a year for up to fifteen years, with the right to take possession sooner in the event of his death. This meant they might be overpaying a little, or underpaying if his life ended quite soon. They agreed, and also gave him a charge account at the Ellicott store, where his purchases could simply be deducted from what they owed him. In a sense, he felt, this would be like collecting some of his money just by making necessary purchases. It turned out that the Ellicotts had to pay less than $800 before Banneker's life ended. But for those last years, the deal gave him peace of mind, and it even facilitated one momentous purchase—a fine pocket watch of his own, carrying with it the memory of that borrowed watch that he had once taken apart and reassembled in the course of learning to make his celebrated wooden clock.

One hidden price he paid for this peace was a nagging sense of guilt at letting go of land that the family had won with such effort. He wrote defensively in his diary, pointing out that his sisters, Minta Black and Molly Morten, were comfortably married and their children were well started in life, and they had no great need of an inheritance from him. In fact, it is believed that the daughters of these sisters did eventually divide what was left of the old Timber Poynt property. And one mitigating fact made Benjamin feel a little better about his decision to sell: His nephew Greenbury Morten, who was Molly's son, bought twenty acres of the land around the time of the "annuity" deal with the Ellicotts. This young Morten, incidentally, was a bright young man who went on to work a good many years at Ellicott's Mills. He also had considerable initiative and took an active part in the affairs of the community. His Aunt Minta once said that Greenbury had asserted his rights as a free black so effectively that he had even dared to step up and vote in elections. If she was right about that, his status as a free black landowner and his general character apparently made him so respected that no one was inclined to challenge him. On the other hand, since Minta had once said similar unusual things about Banneker's access to civil rights, it is possible that she habitually stated what she fondly preferred to believe.

Banneker now had the pleasurable existence of a person who no longer has to work, yet does not actually retire because his main interest is a solo activity that never ceases to absorb him. Although he suffered arthritic pain that hampered movement, it did not prevent him, on most days, from taking long walks with the aid of a cane. And he continued to study the heavens through his telescope, which he had mounted next to a window, allowing him to work indoors on almost every cloudless night. The modern discoveries that astonish even the most advanced cosmologists would have been new to him, of course, but by no means hard for him to believe or to incorporate into his notion of the universe. He had always assumed there were spaces and distances and objects out there that dwarfed anything man could imagine. It is not hard to understand why many human beings find it daunting and even terrifying to contemplate the awesome space through which our little Earth hurtles. Banneker was one of those who got just the opposite sensation from looking upward. The more we learned, he felt, the smaller we would seem in terms of our own relative size; but this, by proving the Creator to be ever more majestic, he believed, should give us an increasing sense of trust and security.

More and more of his time was devoted to reading, and he had been able to buy several books of his own, while still relying on the many that were loaned to him by the Ellicotts. But he specially treasured the first book he ever bought for himself, a fine edition of the Holy Bible that he had acquired at age thirty-two. It is not known whether Molly Banneka's Bible, the one she had used in teaching little Benjamin to read, had somehow been lost or had gone to another family member. The idea of having a family Bible must have been very important to Banneker in his early thirties, for it had been a costly purchase, and he soon started inscribing important dates into it. He also loved the common sense in it, especially some of the Old Testament teachings. He was no "fundamentalist," in the modern sense, for he would never have imagined that any human being knew how the Creator made the world or peopled it. But he thought it to be a guide to living that could make this a much finer existence if the lessons were applied.

With all that, he kept resisting affiliation with any established church. For a time, he thought seriously that he should align himself with one of the great faiths, and he began a series of visits to various houses of worship with the intention of perhaps making a choice. It was like him to do this kind of methodical research, even though he had been inclined to favor the Quakers all along. Not only was he grateful for the many times when persons of that persuasion had shown him the greatest courtesies, but he also found in their beliefs the logic and justice that he imagined the Creator wished to see. It is not clear, however, whether he ever formally joined the Quakers. It has been suggested that his reluctance to take up any formal affiliation was due to an attachment to the faith of his African forebears. This is possible, of course, but seems unlikely, for it was never mentioned in anything he wrote. Thoughts he expressed make it likelier that the very idea of becoming part of any group, be it a church or a political party, seemed to him to swallow up an individual's free intelligence, obligating him or her to surrender the right of dissent from whatever the community mind might dictate on any given subject.

Along with thoughts that reached out to the vastness of time and space, Banneker was now keeping up with community activity in the relatively small Patapsco region, the recently activated capital of Washington, D.C., that he had helped to create, and the states around it. He had read a great deal about the memorable visit of the French duc de La Rochefoucauld, whose views about the new nation were incisive enough to still be quoted today. Noting the speculative scramble to make profits by buying up lots around the Washington area, the Frenchman laughed off the rampant criticism of the new capital and predicted a great future for it. On the other hand, La Roche-foucauld was much less sanguine when he learned that the adjoining town of Upper Marlboro, the seat of Prince Georges County, Maryland, had more slaves than free persons—12,000 in an overall population of 22,000. Strangely, Banneker thought, some wise foreign travelers were quick to see anomalies that America's own leaders, once so foresighted, were now choosing to overlook.

Another of these distinguished tourists was Baron Alexander von Humboldt, a young Prussian scientist and explorer who came after making a geographical survey of Latin America. He was lionized by society and adored by all the ladies, but the attention never distracted him from observing how great this new land could become. In 1804, Europeans were inclined to think themselves to be at the true center of the world, fascinated but not at all rivaled by the vastness of America. Humboldt, however, foresaw that a glorious capital city would grow from the "vast Serbonian bog" with a population of only 4,500 at that time. What impressed Banneker most was that this young visionary, after saying, "I have come not to see your great rivers and mountains, but to become acquainted with your great men," was reported by a newspaper to have spent several days with "the famous astronomer-cartographer, Andrew Ellicott."

Banneker's leisurely existence was sporadically troubled by a succession of physical threats and disturbing dreams that he recorded in more and more detail. His journal pages for those years contain numerous examples of instances when unknown persons were heard outside his cabin and even when gunshots were fired very close to his door. There is no overt mention of fear at those times, but the incidents apparently caused him to have a series of very disturbed dreams, showing that the risk he was running troubled his mind more than he wanted to admit to himself, or so the laconic tone of his accounts would indicate. One example, dated April 29, 1798, reads: "Came two black men with a gun in my inclose and discharged it a few [illegible] from me. I being very unwell, could not pursue them to find who they were." The fact that they were black proves nothing. The tactics of his racist enemies during his late years and after his death would indicate they were the sort of persons who might have paid quite innocent blacks to make a threatening foray of this kind. And there was a footnote on a later page, saying: "The night of 27 November 1802 my house was violently broken open and several articles taken out." These were startling experiences in the placid area he had known so long. And he guessed them to be racially motivated, for the old anger of neighbors who had rented land from him was a thing of the past, whereas the hatred of anti-abolitionists he knew to be ineradicable. Banneker made no mention of even considering a complaint to the sheriff's office or the Ellicott City police. Prominent as he was, he had to wonder which side the authorities were on in the case of racists.

The bad dreams may have been a direct consequence of this feeling of being threatened, although it will require study by experts in dreams to interpret the increasing number, complexity, and violence of his dreams in these later years. As noted earlier, he had been recording dreams in his journal for a long time, and he seemed to remember them in great detail when he woke. But now they became so weird and often bizarre that historians have speculated that they were probably fictional stories. In so concluding, they are apparently failing to note a difference between his fictitious tales about dreams when he was in his thirties and the very real dreams of these older years. Given the fact that he liked to earn money by writing and had contacts with leading printers in his later years, he now had no reason to invent wild plots if he wasn't going to attempt to turn them into saleable fiction. Unlike the contrived dream stories of younger years, these accounts have the incoherence of actual bad dreams, recorded for himself alone. He laboriously put the details into his journal, with no attempt to make them known to a larger audience.

The case for believing that Banneker really had these dreams and recorded them as he remembered them is strengthened by the fact that several such accounts break off with an indication that he forgot the rest. One tells of his holding a fawn or young deer with white hair that is "beautiful to behold." But he clips the tip of an ear, in order to recognize it if he should ever see it again. The fawn cries like a child, filling him with sorrow. He takes wool from a garment and wipes blood from the wound, then is holding the fawn on his knees. There is a short, confused sentence about getting some milk for the fawn, but then come the words, "My dream left me. B. Banneker."

Another dream begins disturbingly:

Being weary holing for corn, I laid down on my bed and fell into a deep sleep and dreamed that I had a child in my arms and was viewing the back part of its head where it had been sore, and I found it was healed with a hole through the skin and Scull bone and came out at forehead, that I could see very distinctly through the child's head the hole being large enough to receive an ordinary finger—

I called some woman to see the strange sight, and she put her spectacles on and saw it, and she asked me if I had previously lanced that place in the child's head. I answered in the affirmative.

N.B. the Child is well as any other.

Perhaps the weirdest of Banneker's dreams, seeming to show the combination of mental stress and religious impulses he was experiencing, was recounted in the following entry on December 13, 1797:

I dreamed I saw something passing by my door to and fro. When I attempted to go to the door, it vanished, then reappeared two or three [*sic*]. At length, I let in the infernal spirit and he told me that he had been concerned with a woman by the name of Beckey Freeman (I never heard the name as I remember). By some means we fell into a skirmish, and I threw him behind the fire and endeavored to burn him up, but all in vain as I know not what became of him. His feet were circular or rather globular and did not exceed an inch and a half in diameter. But while I held him in the fire, he said something respecting he was able to stand it, but I forget his words.

B. Banneker

It is not certain that the term "infernal spirit" means that Banneker was wrestling with the devil. Since there is no capitalization of those two words, they could have been a generic expression, rather than the devil himself. But the spirit's remark that he was able to stand the fire does indicate that he is either Lucifer or one of his close accomplices. And Banneker's inclusion of this as an item worthy enough to be in his journal shows that he considered it significant, for he often mentioned having a dream without recording it in detail. It seems plausible that Banneker felt this dream had been caused by real concerns he was having, perhaps about the dangers he was incurring by publishing almanacs. He knew that the pro-slavery forces regarded each new issue as a flagrant and provocative challenge to the existence of slavery. Some of the six almanacs published from 1792 through 1797 contained outspoken words about freedom and injustice. In particular, they aimed ridicule at the self-importance and pomposity of all those who saw themselves as great personages. Banneker was not at all inclined to make a display of bravado, and most times his lifelong prudence seemed to win out over physical courage. But there was something about the process of writing that stiffened his resolve, as if there was a tonic in the act of writing as he pleased. He did not for a moment consider stopping publication until the sales ebbed.

It is at least arguable that these bona fide dreams and their disagreeable themes reflected the disturbed mental state of one who knew that he had many adversaries who wished him silenced or dead. Most of his life had been spent in obscurity, a simple farmer whom no one feared or thought of harming. From the moment he sent the letter to Jefferson, he had known that he might become a marked man. Then came the publicity promoted by the abolitionist societies, and finally the almanacs, actually making him an activist and therefore a combatant. True, the dreams seemed to grow more intense after he had discontinued the almanacs. But he thought there were still enemies who would continue to consider his very existence to be a challenge to their cause. In this, he was right, for the threatening incidents around his cabin went on. When he realized that just stopping publication had not ended the danger, the prospect of being trapped in his cabin with no way out was worse than during the days when fear was at least matched by the excitement of action.

A nighttime visit to Oella and to the area where his cabin had stood makes his fears seem palpable. Even today, with a few lights along the road and a handful of dimly lit houses within two or three hundred yards along the way, the lonely darkness is oppressive. Looking down from his exact cabin site, the soft lights of Elkridge and Ellicott City seem distant, underlining how far a lone occupant would have been from any form of security or assistance. To be a marked man in an easily entered cabin at a time when neighbors were even farther away and darkness was total would have frightened a Roman gladiator. Going to bed each night in a lonely cabin that was not particularly secure must always have been accompanied by the thought of danger lurking out there in the darkness.

18

Ennobled by Flame

Providentially, Banneker never knew a day of great suffering in his last years. More important to this man for whom the ability to think was the main reason for living, he never lost his mental clarity or his curiosity about the world. When he was nearing age seventy-five, his health and physical vigor declining, friends who accompanied him on his long daily walks recalled his lively observations on everything they passed. It was like seeing everything more clearly, with a brighter light shining on it, just to hear his comments.

That was true on October 9, 1806. He and a friend were enjoying a pleasant stroll and commenting on the beautiful fall afternoon when Benjamin began to feel ill. They got back to his cabin just in time, for there he collapsed. He died peacefully within hours.

Two days later, on October 11, his coffin, surrounded by relatives, friends, and even more people from miles around who had often nodded respectfully when they passed him on a road, was lowered into the trench that awaited it at the nearby burial ground. At that very moment—though the mourners would not know it for a half-hour—flames suddenly erupted in his cabin and raged unimpeded, burning the little structure to the ground and consuming nearly everything inside. Included were the wooden clock and most of the journals and other papers that held the thoughts of a remarkable lifetime. Just a few things survived by sheer luck because they had been accidentally returned to the Ellicotts along with some books and instruments that Banneker had borrowed. Saved was a manuscript journal he had kept for some years, and it was precious, even though not from his most productive period. It is clear that innumerable earlier ideas about astronomy and other sciences were reduced to ashes, because Banneker had referred to them in later notations. Most of those would undoubtedly appear elementary today; it was not a permanent loss to science, but, based on the rather few observations we do have from Banneker, it is certain that they were not at all simplistic in his day. The real loss to human understanding was the obliteration of additional proof that great mental ability has nothing to do with race. All the burned notes would have strengthened the evidence that his ideas were original and independent. They might well have encouraged the abolitionists to publish a biography of Banneker's life, making such a volume an indestructible banner for their cause. But with so little material available, no one thought of taking on such a task. This delayed, at least by many decades, the first credible account of black mental abilities to reach a broad public audience.

A handful of remarkable clergymen had been preaching about this subject for years, in Pennsylvania, France, and England, but their writing was too far ahead of their time to be widely accepted. The abolitionists who said such things were often regarded as mere faddists in pursuit of their hobby. Some of them were even mistrusted by blacks, who thought they had a social or political agenda of their own. There were obituary notices about Banneker in several newspapers, which was then a rare honor for a black person, and there was a laudatory article by the faithful Senator McHenry, but these echoing reminders of a great man soon faded. The several thousand people who had bought Banneker's almanac could have made a difference in the course of time, but when the publication ceased, natural attrition dried up the interest.

That, of course, was precisely the reason for the fire. Some friends in Ellicott City and in the Banneker neighborhood (which was just about to be incorporated with the name of Oella) said in hushed tones that the fire must have been a mystical event, a sign that the heavens were lighting a memorial in his honor, and other emotional remarks of that nature. Benjamin Banneker would have known better. He would have seen that all his fears and eerie dreams of recent years had been based on very real evil forces that had nothing to do with mysticism. He would have said in his balanced way that he was fortunate that the people who were bad enough to do this had not been quite bad enough to burn the place while he was sleeping in it.

While political leaders who would really have preferred an end to slavery did not feel strongly enough about the issue to push hard against the forces that might have challenged their power and torn the country apart, the cabin-burners were a different breed. They were dedicated racists, committed to slavery as an institution. Somehow—and this was a blessing—they were not quite bold enough to take a life that threatened to undermine their position. Perhaps they were clever enough to know that creating a martyr might harm their cause. But when an unoccupied cabin contained flammable objects with added proof of just what they wanted to suppress, their course was clear. It was all too easy to bury the man's traces on the same day the man himself was buried.

The cabin was so thoroughly razed that the area was hardly searched. Two attempts were made to put a small marker on the

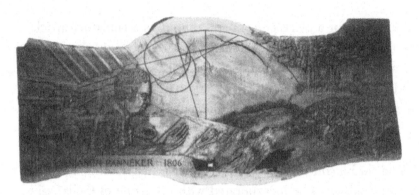

Wood-cut mural in solid walnut in the Howard County Offices, Ellicott City, Maryland, executed by John Levering in 1977. Shows the subject studying in his cabin, with symbols of his scientific research around him and a view of the tobacco farm outdoors.

site, but it was destroyed by vandals both times. Nearly a half-century after his death, when the feelings that led to the Civil War were stirring, a few articles about Banneker appeared and lectures about him were given, especially at the Maryland Historical Society. Very late in the nineteenth century, Martha Ellicott Tyson, the daughter of George Ellicott, dictated her invaluable memoir about Banneker to her daughter. A very old lady by that time, she had a vivid memory of the man and, as noted earlier, was driven to tell her story by the recollection that her father had always wanted to write this himself. Nothing else, except Banneker's own letters and notes, can compare with Martha Tyson's firsthand account.

Not until the early 1970s, 165 years after his death, was there a small public funding to memorialize Banneker's remarkable career. A researcher named John McGrain did extensive work with land records and found the boundaries of his one hundred–acre farm. In the mid-1980s, the Baltimore County Department of Recreation and Parks purchased what had been identified as the Banneker Farmstead, along with some forty acres of surrounding land. A Benjamin Banneker Historical Park was established and a small marble building erected. Regrettably, its artifacts and other contents are few. More archaeological digging and a search for items that may be in collectors' hands are projected.

~

The traces of a black person's existence were tantalizingly vague in the eighteenth century—no mailing address, no club memberships, almost no correspondence, hardly anything recorded in public documents. There are stretches in Benjamin Banneker's life when it seems that we hardly have the subject in our sights. But in the end, we know the real man very well—know Banneker better than we know most modern celebrities who show a great deal of skin but hardly a clue as to their real character. His life was a quest for a certain kind of beauty, the elegance of perfect balance. He saw balance as the true and enduring beauty, because imbalance was destined to cause failure. That is why he was passionate about time, a watch, a wooden clock, the punctual new time-saving machinery at Ellicott's Mills. A good many technically minded persons have this feeling for the mechanisms they work with. But Banneker applied his love of balance to the whole physical world. When he turned one of Andrew Ellicott's fine instruments to locate a star, he forgot the cold and the arthritis, for he was seeing another cog in the Great Machine, and its total reliability was breathtaking. To look at a balanced mechanism and relate it to a passion for the balanced universe takes an unusual mind, though not at all sui generis. There are other minds that see beauty in a principle and share Banneker's ability to project the principle they love to other spheres. What is rarest of all, however, is Banneker's way of converting this mechanical ideal into a philosophy

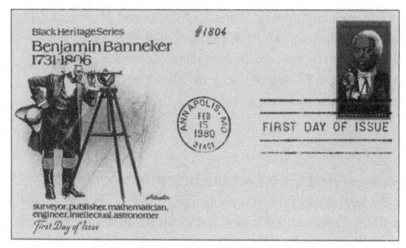

A first-day cover of the Benjamin Banneker stamp, issued by the U.S. Postal Service on February 15, 1980.

of life. If there were an ideology called "Bannekerism," it would say: He saw the beauty of the perfectly balanced mechanism as a pattern that was meant to be copied in human behavior.

It follows from this belief that the two words "peace" and "justice" were not, to him, the banal sounds that are usually swallowed mindlessly and left undigested. He thought of them as literally the conditions necessary to make the mechanism of a community or a nation function as it should. If he had heard George S. Patton's lurid praise of war as his idea of great beauty and majesty, Banneker would have understood the general's love for the tanks and other machines of battle, but turned away as sadly as any sensitive person who hears his own ideal mangled.

Peace—people working in harmony—was to him not just the best way, but the only way. A democracy that works well was, to Banneker, the epitome of beautiful organization, specifically because it calls for so many "moving parts" to operate while being conscious of how they affect each other. That was why he could worry about how his letter to Jefferson had affected the writer of such perfect words about democracy, even if the man had fallen so far short of his own language. Banneker conveyed this feeling of fairness and balance so thoroughly in all his conversations that ladies always spoke of how "gentle" he was, men at Ellicott's Mills called his observations (even on subjects that were new to him) "damned interesting," and both groups' eyes lit up when he appeared.

APPENDIX I

The Dogon Ancestors

The Dogon people are thought to have fled from the headwaters of the Niger between the tenth and thirteenth centuries to escape from pressure to convert to Islam, and the refuge of a great escarpment that is part of the Bandiagara cliffs has kept them intact and rather isolated. They live today, as they have for centuries, mainly by raising grain, especially millet, and they trade their products with another Mali community, the Fulani people, who specialize in dairy products.

Several things make Banneker's relationship to the Dogon especially significant. They have a complicated theology and cosmology that is based on an elaborate numerical formula. Even before most other advanced peoples, they saw the structure of the world as being related to the human body. The hand, for example, made the number 8 central to this, apparently based on the number of fingers without the thumbs. So 8 and its multiples were basic, just as 10 and the decimal system were basic for the Romans. They believe that the old Nummo spirit, architect of the world, laid out eight covenant stones that outlined the human soul. He also provided eight ancestors as progenitors of the eight Dogon clans that would make up human society. Very elderly Dogon say that when men began trading, they counted in eights; and even when the French came as colonists and talked of "hundreds" (or *centaines*), the Dogon considered that to mean 80.

Serious researchers speak of an "indigenous literacy" among the Dogon, a system of writing that predated the coming of Europeans. They have also found that Dogon technology has long covered mining, metal processing, cotton planting and textiles, food storage, architecture, erosion control, and irrigation.

There are indications that the Dogon people knew long before the Europeans that Earth orbits around the sun. Some experts in African studies are convinced that they also knew about other planets and even worlds beyond the solar system. Those who insist this is so have tried to explain it by showing that the Dogon may have come upon the Egyptians' way of using crystals to shape lenses that could serve as simple telescopes. There are doubters who say that even if this were so, there is no such lens arrangement that gives enough magnification to account for the disputed belief that Dogons were centuries ahead in knowing that the "Dog Star" has a unique twinkle because it is actually a double star (called Sirius A and Sirius B). They supposedly even knew that the interplay of their two orbits took either fifty or sixty years to be completed.

The disbelievers would appear to be the more credible—until it is realized that in the late 1700s, Benjamin Banneker reportedly said Sirius was both his favorite star and his lucky star, and called it a double star many years before professional scientists of the advanced world confirmed that fact. Some have used this to assert that he mystically inherited this knowledge, as if it had been transmitted through the DNA. But the simpler explanation would appear to be that Grandfather Banneka had talked of certain ancient wisdom to Molly, who had passed it along to Benjamin when he was a boy. Banneker may later have adapted it to fit his own updated astronomical thoughts.

This finding has the multiple function of pinpointing the location of Banneker's hitherto-unknown African roots, for no African people other than the Dogon are known to have had any special interest in the star called Sirius. It does not, of course, reveal the identity of the ancient Dogon who had the original insight about the dual nature of Sirius. Since it is provable that the difference between these A and B stars is invisible without magnification many times greater than any

African people are known to have had, the only explanation would have to be that a great early Dogon thinker, having noted a wobbly twinkle different from any other, simply had the astonishing insight that two stars locked in a strange dance might be producing such an effect. It was, after all, just such a capacity for pure reason that made Benjamin Banneker a finer astronomer than many who had much superior equipment.

A less exact but very telling personal trait ties Banneker to the Dogon. Europeans who have lived among the Dogon describe them in the very same terms that were so often applied to Banneker by contemporaries. Antonin Potovski, a French photographer who has worked and taught in Mali for some years, has written, "Dogon teenagers rarely mess around. From a very early age, they are exposed to the hard work crucial for survival in a semi-arid environment. Since the villagers' well-being depends on them and their involvement in a host of daily chores, the classic problems encountered by urban teenagers are not felt here." He calls the Dogon "one of the world's most extraordinary cultures." Today, as in antiquity, they are known as particularly dignified and orderly people. Even through the vicissitudes of colonialism, this remained a constant. And other groups in Mali, including those who have had commercial disputes with the Dogon, still speak of them that way today. Further, they are known to dislike all forms of disagreement, always opting to stress compromise over confrontation, tending to gain respect by the moderation of their arguments. That is exactly what Banneker's acquaintances always said about him. But just as the ancient Dogon people had a breaking point that made them leave the Niger headwaters and move to the rocky escarpment of the Bandiagara to protect their own beliefs, Banneker was finally prompted to turn away from quiet living within an unjust system and to confront its leaders with a historic protest.

A Significant Similarity

Benjamin Franklin was just twenty-six years old when he became a national figure by compiling the first edition of *Poor Richard's Almanac*. Benjamin Banneker, who was only a year old at that time, did not publish the almanac that had been forming in his mind for so long until he was sixty-one. Yet they were brothers and virtually twins in talents and in character. Some persons who had seen them both even noticed that Banneker, as he aged, began to look like Franklin, with the same portliness, very short neck, and benign expression.

It is strange that a comparison of Franklin and Banneker has never been noted, for the similarities of their mental processes are astonishing. Although they never met, both men developed a parallel manner of analyzing problems and communicating their conclusions. Both had a unique way of discovering scientific truths and then stating them so simply that they came to seem "obvious" to ordinary minds; they appeared to accomplish this effortlessly, but only because both had such powerful minds and disciplined approaches that what others regarded as onerous mental effort was as natural as breathing. Both also shared a wisdom about human affairs that they could communicate in a way that quickly struck others as elementary common sense. They made distasteful medicine seem palatable.

How little race has to do with mental ability is reconfirmed by the fact that both were universal geniuses, their rare abilities going beyond any single specialty. Franklin was the only person among the Founding Fathers who deserves that title. He and Banneker combined superior intuition in the sciences with an inborn mastery of philosophical principles and a grasp of how civilization can be advanced. Thomas Jefferson has been spoken of as a genius, but, in fact, his array of talents would appear to have been more a matter of great intellectual interest and facility in taking up many subjects with an amateur's enthusiasm.

Other leaders who fashioned the Revolution and the establishment of a nation were very great men, but they were using established wisdom as their guide. They stood in awe of the aged "Dr. Franklin," as he was known after receiving an honorary L.L.D. degree from the Scottish University of St. Andrews, who could often settle a dispute with a wise thought that had not occurred to the rest. This was a man who, when his brother John was dying in Boston because doctors knew no way to reach his abdominal tumor, invented a simple instrument (now known as a flexible catheter) that made the operation possible; this same self-taught man was credited with saving the life of Lord Cardross when he advised against a physician's decision to use "blistering" as a treatment for his fever.

The two Benjamins shared a conviction that writing was a passkey to success, and both took justifiable pride in their own skill. That many of Franklin's writings were on scientific subjects written in fine language that is accessible to any average reader is well known. Similarly, there were times when Banneker used simple but elegant language in this same way. In a memorable piece of writing in the 1792 almanac, for example, he achieved three objectives in a single essay: a remarkable picture of the cosmos, a perceptive view of the humans who inhabit it, and finally a shattering philosophical judgment about their pitiful egotism. It is arguable that no unschooled, self-educated person of any race or country ever expressed the nuances of his thought with more perfect choice of words. Even apart from the content, the vocabulary and construction have a quality that ranks Banneker with the fine American writers of any era. Part of the essay shows how gracefully he coupled and conveyed his observations:

The sun, though seemingly smaller than the dial it illuminates, is abundantly larger than this whole earth, on which so many lofty mountains rise and such vast oceans roll. A line extending from side to side through the center of that resplendent orb would measure more than eight hundred thousand miles: A girdle formed to go round its circumference would require a length of millions. Were its solid contents to be estimated, the account would overwhelm our understanding and be almost beyond the power of language to express. . . .

This sun, with all its attendant planets, is but a very little part of the grand machine of the universe; every star, though in appearance no bigger than the diamond that glitters upon a lady's ring, is really a vast globe, like the sun in size and in glory; no less spacious, no less luminous, than the radiant source of the day: So that every star is not barely a world, but the centre of a magnificent system; has a retinue of worlds, irradiated by its beams, and revolving around its attractive influence, all of which are lost to our sight in unmeasurable wilds of ether. That the stars appear like so many diminutive and scarce distinguishable points is owing to their immense and inconceivable distance. Immense and inconceivable indeed it is, since a ball, shot from the loaded cannon, and flying with unabated rapidity, must travel at this impetuous rate almost seven hundred thousand years, before it could reach the nearest of these twinkling luminaries.

While beholding this vast expanse, I learn my own extreme meanness. I would also discover the abject littleness of all terrestrial things. What is the earth, with all her ostentatious scenes, compared with this astonishing grand furniture of the skies? What but a dim speck, hardly perceivable in the map of the universe? It is observed by a very judicious writer, that if the sun himself . . . was extinguished, and all the host of planetary worlds which move about him were annihilated, they would not be missed by an eye that can take on the whole compass of nature any more than a grain of sand upon the sea-shore. The bulk of which they consist and the space which they occupy is so exceedingly little in comparison of the whole that their loss would leave scarce a blank in the immensity of God's works. If then, not our globe only, but this whole system, be so very diminutive, what is a kingdom or a country? What are a few lordships, or the so much admired patrimonies of those who are styled wealthy? When I measure them with my own little pittance, they swell into proud bloated dimensions. But when I take the universe for my standard, how scanty is their size, how contemptible their figure! They shrink into pompous nothings.

There is a tone and a clarity in Banneker's serious essays that have an astonishing kinship with some of Benjamin Franklin's writings. Both these men—almost entirely on their own—had acquired enormous vocabularies mainly from books and then applied some innate sense of taste and proportion to shape all those thousands of words into discourses that could appeal to many levels of society. They never made the kind of mistake that so often betrays uneducated persons who use great words inappropriately. On the contrary, their word selection is absolutely meticulous. Franklin, simply because of his race, had far more sources, for he was able to glean and hone information by aggressively seeking out and listening to the leading people of the age. Banneker was, if anything, the more remarkable because he lacked this opportunity. But it is amazing how similarly both Benjamins crafted words that appealed to simple farmers or housewives, yet could make many an intellectual pause, reflect, and take their thoughts to heart.

From a very early age, both had grasped for more learning, also on their own, charting programs for self-improvement, one skipping meals to buy books and skipping sleep to practice his writing style (Franklin, in his teens), or setting himself the goal of discovering at least one new principle of physics for himself each day (Banneker, in his youth). They seemed very different in their ambitions, yet both valued financial independence very highly, and both held prudence, the classical idea of moderation, to be one of the greatest virtues.

Although Franklin had the worldly advantage of being white, he was a poor boy who worked as a lowly apprentice after less than two years of schooling. Banneker may have had one year in a schoolroom, or perhaps he had only a friendly teacher who loaned him books.

Franklin was once youthfully naive in believing the empty promises of Pennsylvania's governor, Sir William Keith, about a financial opportunity he would arrange for him in England. Upon arrival there, Franklin found himself both jobless and penniless, but the need to use his printing abilities urgently in order to earn a living gave him no time to be depressed. Banneker is thought to have made his own youthful travel blunder when he was misled by loose talk about the chances for great tobacco prices in Baltimore, and allowed rashness to win over his usual good judgment. In his case, it was the discovery of new scientific facts that quickly overcame his despair. But both Benjamins learned their lesson so well that prudence became a lifelong trait.

Where the similarity becomes most visible is in the tendency to think about and to write down bits of advice for living, which they first intended for themselves, but then went on to offer for publication. At a very young age, Franklin was dashing off such homey doggerel as:

For age and want
Save while you may.
No morning sun
Lasts the whole day

Banneker said almost exactly the same thing in prose form. One of the many treatises on the subject of time published in his own almanac revealed a thought he had cherished since his youth. He interrupted the scientific aspects of time to point out: "Many who accurately mark the course of time appear to have little sensibility of the decline of life. Every man has something to do which he neglects;

every man has faults to conquer which he delays to combat . . . Let him that desires to see others happy make haste to give while his gifts can be enjoyed . . . and let him who proposes his own happiness reflect that while he forms his purposes the day rolls on and 'the night cometh when no man can work.'"

Both of these men impressed women with their personable charm and speech. In Franklin's case, it was courtly sophistication; in Banneker's, it was gentleness. Both men were very sociable and fine conversationalists. There was one difference in that Franklin was a sexual adventurer at times, though he quickly developed a cautious streak about his relationships after a wild youthful fling in London. There was a great deal of flirtatious talk, especially in Paris, but apparently no real liaisons.

Although very successful with spoken language, both men held their tongues and thought at great length before speaking when any issue was at stake. Thomas Jefferson said long afterward, "I served with General Washington in the legislature of Virginia before the Revolution and during it with Dr. Franklin in Congress. I never heard either of them speak ten minutes at a time, nor to any but the main point which was to decide the question." Just a brief remark by the aged Franklin when the Declaration of Independence was being discussed brought about the great phrase, "We hold these truths to be self-evident . . . " He once dashed off a bombastic letter to a friend in the British government whose policies were bad for the American colonies, but held it for weeks, then rewrote it in less heavy-handed form. Banneker deliberated for days before venturing a criticism of a famous astronomer's error in calculation. And he thought even longer and harder about the accusatory letter that he finally sent to Thomas Jefferson.

But they both were to undergo great changes when their lives went on to the phase of maximum recognition and excitement. It is almost uncanny how the two Benjamins—some fifteen years apart—both discarded their cherished prudence and uncapped a well of risk-taking courage that put principle above every other consideration.

"Men of seventy seldom make revolutions," as Franklin's greatest biographer, Carl Van Doren, wrote. But it might equally be said that an elderly black man who was reveling in his new prominence and the success of an amazing publishing venture was acting in a revolutionary way when he risked his all on a quixotic challenge to the powers that be. Franklin, although almost a full generation older than most of the other political leaders, became an all-out supporter of vigorous protest against British policies toward the colonies—protest plus military preparedness in order to be ready for war if the Crown refused to heed American demands. Thought to be the man who told other patriots, "We must all hang together, or we shall surely hang separately," he knew that he was risking everything, including his life, in the stand that he took. Banneker, when he was in the seventh decade of a cautiously lived life, may have taken an even more frightening risk when he suddenly called the Founding Fathers frauds over the slavery question. Since no prominent black person had ever taken such an overt step against the white establishment, he could have no idea whether he would ultimately "hang alone."

These are not even half the parallels that could be made in comparing the two persons. It is as if they had been born nonidentical twins, with an extroverted one raised in a cool northern climate and a quiet-living one browned by an equatorial sun.

And carrying that fanciful analogy a little further, the white northern twin was a slave owner early in life. But as early as 1751, long before his Southern twin lashed out against such infamy, Benjamin Franklin had turned sharply against slavery. He suggested establishing a school for blacks in Philadelphia in 1758, then took over the presidency of the Pennsylvania Society for Promoting the Abolition of Slavery in 1787. In his last years, he also headed a new and much-needed Society For the Relief of Free Negroes Unlawfully Held in Bondage.

Of course, it might be said, Benjamin Franklin could change in that way because he was long past any role in practical politics. Washington, Jefferson, and the other leaders would have thought it a grave

threat to the existence of the young nation to let the example of Benjamin Banneker demonstrate how very capable of mental effort a
black person could be. But the argument is not valid. Franklin had
turned against slavery during the years when he *was* politically active.
And even in his last years, it was not because he had lost interest in
the survival of the United States that he took up and publicized his
anti-slavery attitude. Just the reverse. He did not believe that political
expediency in a bad cause is either expedient or good politics. He
broke with his own son, who had become governor of New Jersey,
because they disagreed on the policies that certain issues called for.
And, like Banneker, he opposed injustice to Native Americans as well
as to blacks. He wrote, "It has appeared to me that almost every war
between the Indians and whites has been occasioned by some injustice
of the latter towards the former."

Sources

Archives of the State of Maryland, Annapolis, MD

Banneker-Douglass Museum, Annapolis, MD

Benjamin Banneker Memorial, Oella, MD

Ms. Beulah Buckner, student of local history, Ellicott City, MD

Ms. Wylene Burch, Founder-Director of the Howard County Center of African-American History, near Ellicott City, MD

Enoch Pratt Free Library, Baltimore, MD

Free Library of Philadelphia, PA

Historical Society of Howard County (Mary Mannix, Library Director), Ellicott City, MD

Historical Society of Maryland, Baltimore, MD

Historical Society of Pennsylvania, Philadelphia, PA

Historical Society of Washington, D.C. (Gail Redman, Librarian)

Mr. Samuel Hopkins, Baltimore, MD, historian, descendant of George Ellicott

Howard County Tourism Council (Melissa Arnold, Coordinator), Ellicott City, MD

Dr. James Huckenpahler, historian, Washington, D.C.

Ms. Victoria Huckenpahler, writer, Washington, D.C.

Ms. Gwen Marable, descendant of Minta Bannaky

Ms. Alice McGill, author, Columbia, MD

New York Public Library, New York, NY

Professional Surveyors Association, Frederick, MD (Mark Cheves, Jackie Cheves)

Ms. Ann Ryder, Coordinator, Howard County Offices, Ellicott City, MD

The Schomburg Center for Research in Black Culture, affiliated with the New York Public Library, New York, NY

U.S. Naval Observatory, Washington, D.C.
Geoff Chester, Public Affairs Officer
Steve Dick, Historian

Ms. Jean Walsh, Catonsville, MD, student of local history

Washingtoniana Room, Martin Luther King Memorial Library, Washington, D.C.

General Source Notes

1 The Prince and the Convict

Extended talks with Mr. Samuel Hopkins of Baltimore and with Ms. Beulah Buckner and Ms. Ann Ryder of the Ellicott City area were especially valuable in preparing this and other early chapters that cover the part of Banneker's life for which precise information is scarce and a great deal of informed deduction is required.

Truly invaluable in this and several other chapters was Martha Ellicott Tyson's personal memoir of Banneker. Hers is the only written account that has memories dating back to Banneker's own lifetime, as Mrs. Tyson had childhood experiences of the great friendship between her father, George Ellicott, and Banneker. Her own remembrance, dictated to her daughter when Mrs. Tyson was very old, was further enhanced by the reminiscences of her mother, Elizabeth Ellicott, who had also been an admirer of Banneker and an adviser to him on some important occasions. In her own right, Mrs. Tyson had been one of the founders of Swarthmore College and of the Patapsco Female Institute. Frederick Douglass later wrote to Anne Tyson Kirk, Mrs. Tyson's daughter, complimenting her for the memoir she had written for her mother, saying, "We need such examples of mental industry and success, as I believe the life of Banneker furnishes."

Especially helpful, too, in these early chapters were Silvio Bedini's painstakingly researched biography, *Benjamin Banneker*, and two useful studies of Banneker's probable ancestors, *Dogon*, by Chukwuma Azuonye, and *Africa Counts*, by Claudia Zaslavsky.

2 Lessons, Precious and Painful

Further discussions with Mr. Hopkins and Ms. Ryder continued to be of great value here, and they can be assumed to apply to many of the early chapters. Talks with librarians and board members of the Historical Society of Howard County and Ms. Gwen Marable, a direct descendant of Banneker's sister Minta, gave helpful insights into the mists that envelop his youth, as did Shirley Graham's book titled *Your Most Humble Servant.* (See the "Special Note" below for important facts about Ms. Graham and her work.) Also, *A Salute to Black Scientists*, from the Black History Publications Series, and other such brief works mentioned in the bibliography were useful in supplying an occasional fact that reinforced the evidence on a questionable point.

3 The Lurking Terror

Discussions about the episodes in this chapter were held with the persons cited above, with Ms. Jean Walsh, a student of the history of her Maryland area, and with Ms. Wylene Burch, Founder-Director of the Howard County Center of African-American History, near Ellicott City, Maryland. Also, the uncertain points made in the Shirley Graham book were carefully discussed with my sources, and weighed to elicit as much valuable information as possible, noting that the abduction of an older companion may or may not have actually happened, but was a useful indication of the kind of terror that lurked in Banneker's mind. At the same time, some clearly fictitious material was eliminated. It should be made clear that these early chapters are not without hard facts. Banneker's ancestry, the family's land acquisitions, the young Benjamin's name on the title to the property, his early brilliance, and the help he received from a Quaker schoolmaster—these and other points are fully credible, and they are reconfirmed by the way they connect with his known later life.

4 A Door Opens Wider

Microfilms of Banneker's diary and notes, supplied by the Historical Society of Washington, D.C., and additional microfilms from the Historical Society of Maryland, Baltimore, Maryland, began to put me on entirely solid ground. The firm evidence that Banneker constructed a remarkable wooden clock at this point in his life makes it clear that some anecdotes, such as the disastrous Baltimore trip and the fortunate meeting with a person who introduced him to ideas that fired his thoughts, had some basis in fact.

5   The Great Unknown

Later diary entries obtained from the historical societies noted above gave evidence that Banneker was returning to diary writing after a long lapse. These also showed that his only writing during those lost years had been the long and apparently fictional accounts of dreams like the example given in this chapter. This departure from scientific interest, and its replacement with imaginary dreams, seems to have been the basis for Shirley Graham's lurid tale of a tragic romance. And the modern local sources who express belief in such a romance appear to be merely recalling Ms. Graham's account, rather than basing their support on any tangible evidence. Weighing these reasons for disbelief against the fact that there was, indeed, a "great unknown" period, I have been left to conclude that there was nothing romantic or homosexual to account for it and that Banneker was more likely to have been seriously depressed by the frustration of an intellectual curiosity that had no apparent hope of ever being satisfied.

6   Enter the Ellicotts

The background of the Ellicott family, its coming to the Patapsco region, and its sterling record of refusing to own slaves is amply supported by the various historical societies, but especially by the Historical Society of Howard County. Joseph Ellicott's beautiful clock is a documented fact; its role in bringing Banneker and George Ellicott together is less certain, even though it is quite firmly believed by some of the local historians. What is absolutely sure, as told by Ellicott's own daughter, Margaret Tyson, and also by many notes that the two men exchanged, is that George Ellicott was quickly struck by

Banneker's brilliance and that a genuinely close and lasting friendship formed. The many gifts Banneker received—including astronomical instruments and the large worktable he used until the end of this life—are additional proofs.

7 Turning Night into Day

Banneker's new astronomy-oriented daily schedule is indicated in his own journal pages and also by accounts of stories exchanged among neighbors about Banneker's tendency to stay abed late each morning. Banneker's own written words show how avidly he was beginning to turn his celestial observations into early attempts to compose an ephemeris. His journal also shows that he was already entering arithmetical puzzles and jokes that he would later use in his almanacs.

8 The Unfinished Revolution

I have had to employ a certain amount of deduction in asserting that Banneker definitely believed the Founding Fathers planned to abolish slavery if the Revolutionary War was won. There is nothing in writing to prove this, but both he and his sister asserted that he tried to volunteer for military service, and he did finally convert his farm from tobacco to wheat, even though he had considered it a financial risk, after hearing that wheat flour was badly needed for the military effort. A good many other blacks volunteered to bear arms, but most of them did it after being promised freedom and, in some cases, a grant of land. Banneker was already free and a landowner. What motive other than abolition for others could have made him so anxious to see an American victory is hard to imagine. Finally, with foreknowledge of the letter he would write to Thomas Jefferson ten years after the war had ended, his indictment of the Founders for having been so eager to save their own freedom and then continuing to keep others in captivity seems to me to be the burning words of a man who felt betrayed.

9 Attracted to the City

Here again, Banneker's own journal entries, including his notations dealing with purchases from Ellicott's store, become a running document of his new life. Not only he, but also some of the Ellicott employees have left behind written words about how often they saw him in Ellicott City and how interesting they found his comments on the new machinery in Ellicott's Mills.

10 Meanwhile, at Mount Vernon

Some of the account of the Mount Vernon meeting was suggested by material in three books mentioned in the bibliography: *Colonial America, Contest for a Capital,* and *George Washington.* It was then verified by consulting microfilms on Washington, Jefferson, and George Mason at the Historical Society of Washington, D.C. Tapes dealing with proceedings at the Constitutional Convention were also viewed at the same Society.

11 Astonishing Choices

The books *Contest for a Capital* and *Washington: The Indispensable Man* played a role in parts of this chapter dealing with Major L'Enfant. Microfilms and very old records of the Washington Historical Society (tied with ribbons) from the Washingtoniana Room of the Martin Luther King Library, Washington, D.C., gave a graphic picture of how the early Washingtonians felt about their city's progress. The biographies of Banneker by Martha Tyson and Silvio Bedini were consulted in preparing the parts of this chapter dealing with Banneker's role in the survey. An article by Victoria Huckenpahler, "George Washington Dances," provided an unusual way to sense how the stresses of the presidency appeared to cause Washington's rapid decline from an enthusiastic dancer whom Jefferson termed "the most graceful figure that could be seen" to the suddenly aged man who answered an invitation with "Alas! Our dancing days are no more."

12 Back Home to Plant . . . and Publish

After beginning with Martha Tyson's account of Banneker's return from the survey and then discussing that experience in detail with Mr. Samuel Hopkins, I was able to see extensive news clippings from the Library of the Historical Society of Howard County and the Howard County Center of African-American History. These were augmented by old letters from and to Banneker found in Collection Boxes of the Free Library of Philadelphia, including Leon Gardiner Box 5-G f 16, HSP #154 (John Cox to Banneker) and a Banneker letter to the firm of Cox, Parrish, and Wharton.

13 A Declaration of Indignation

Who originated the idea of Banneker's letter to Thomas Jefferson? There is no written note that shows whether it was Banneker himself or perhaps one of the Ellicotts. I do not presume to know the answer, because Banneker was with George Ellicott so often that either of them might well have uttered the thought. I feel very sure, however, that it immediately appealed to Banneker and then went on growing in his mind. It is made clear in the letter itself that he first planned to write a simple covering letter, making the almanac the centerpiece of the mailing. Then the letter took on a life of its own, with one argument after another being added, until it overtook the almanac in importance, making the latter just an all-conquering piece of evidence. The full text of Banneker's letter to Jefferson has never been questioned, and I have seen it in a great many places, since all the historical societies named earlier have it on microfilm. In addition, the entire letter and Jefferson's reply were printed a year later in some editions of Banneker's almanac.

14 A Founder's Crafty Response

Each person can have his or her own opinion about Jefferson's response to Banneker. I do not think I am being harsh in calling it crafty, for there is not a sentence in it that lacks a double meaning. This judgment is not, however, intended to be unfavorable, for I go on to show that the mere fact of sending a courteous answer caused Jefferson real political problems. It was his later personal letter to a friend, deriding Banneker's intelligence, that seems unfeeling and mean-spirited. Everything in this chapter is based on documentary evidence, clearly shown in papers and microfilms in the historical societies that have been previously named.

15 A Place Among the Greats

That Banneker was one of a very small group of astronomers who made any mention of extra-solar planets is made clear by the virtual omission of this subject in each of the books on astronomy named in the bibliography. The same glaring omission occurs in every leading encyclopedia and in histories of astronomical sciences found in the Library of Congress, the Free Library of Philadelphia, and the Technology Division of the Martin Luther King Library, Washington, D.C. A talk with the U.S. Naval Observatory's public affairs officer Geoff Chester and historian Steve Dick brought the reminder that the seventeenth-century Italian monk Giordano Bruno had been burned at the stake for having mentioned the many other worlds that exist in God's universe. They also confirmed that an English writer, Thomas Wright, had published a book in 1750 with a similar thought. Oddly, Wright's theory got most of its attention from the fact that philosopher Immanuel Kant, who never read Wright's book, wrote and talked about it simply on the basis of a press story. Even the most cautious judge of Banneker's accomplishment on this point would, I feel, grant that Banneker's 1791 writings about extra-solar planets (which I believe he had thought about some forty years earlier) made him one of only three persons who had seriously advanced this idea before astronomers with superior equipment gave firmer evidence of it in the nineteenth and twentieth centuries. In this chapter, however, I have also shown why Banneker may be said to have a superior claim among persons who are thinking purely as scientists. If earlier mentions of extra-solar worlds were all faith-based, Banneker's conclusions were apparently the first assertion about multiple worlds based on more modern scientific reasoning.

16 The Sage's Years of Glory

Here again, I am indebted to the historical societies of Maryland and Howard County for access to microfilms of Banneker's own journal, which was saved from the flames only by a fortunate accident, and to comments from persons who had visited his cabin or had seen him at events he attended in his late years.

17 Living Off the Land Again

Information about Banneker's disappointments as a landlord, his sales of land parcels, and his successful "annuity" arrangement with the Ellicotts is based on his journal and on letters found in the historical societies and in the Free Library of Philadelphia.

18 Ennobled by Flame

This final chapter is clearly my own assessment of Banneker's personality after having read so many of his own words that could not all be included in this narrative. I concluded that while many of his thoughts are proof of genius, his character was every bit as important as his intellect. In his case, the two seem to have been so nearly identical that they meet Aristotle's standard: "The life according to intellect is best and pleasantest, since intellect more than anything else *is* man." Although some of his years are obscured by mist, there are enough of his own words to build a rock-solid image of a man who found the right road to take at every critical intersection of his life. Thought and reasoning and intellectual discovery were his amusement, but he knew that survival, being essential to the others, held the highest priority. So, as a Dogon, he tried to arrange his life in a way that would let him enjoy the mental delights that were a joy until the end. But the fact that his last fifteen years were lived in a most un-Dogon-like duel with deadly enemies shows how deeply he cared for the freedom of his race and, indeed, of all his fellow Americans.

Appendix I   The Dogon Ancestors

The books *Africa Counts* and *Dogon*, included in the Bibliography, were a principal source of information about the group that I have identified as Banneker's probable ancestors. I have also had the good fortune to meet a number of persons from Mali—one at Sacred Heart Adult Education Center, Washington, D.C., where I am a volunteer teacher of writing—and others whose jobs in Washington have brought us into contact. Several of these have brightened when I asked them about the Dogon, not only confirming what I had read in books, but telling me how much the Dogon continue to be admired in Mali.

Appendix II   A Significant Similarity

My comparison of Benjamin Franklin's character to Banneker's began with a long interest that I have had in Franklin and continued with a rereading of Carl Van Doren's great biography, *Benjamin Franklin*. Among other accounts in which I found additional points of interest was *The Private Franklin*, by Claude-Anne Lopez and Eugenia W. Herbert.

Special Note

Shirley Graham (Du Bois)'s book on Banneker has been generally dismissed as a "romanticized biography," because it contains dialogue and dramatic scenes that no twentieth-century author could conceivably have known. She herself hinted that she had considerably embellished certain situations "within the framework of facts that I believe to be true," as she stated it. The fact that her book features many imagined dialogues is evidence that she was not even aiming for a standard biographical format. On closer examination, however, I have found that Ms. Graham did a great deal more research than her detractors have believed. Most of the sources she cites are verifiable, and most of the conclusions she has drawn from them are reasonable. She was a skillful writer who turned the facts into a very readable story, inexact in detail, but probably conveying correct impressions. Her marriage to W.E.B. Du Bois late in that activist's life showed that she might have heard word-of-mouth accounts, which can be enlightening, even if not precisely factual. The close family relationship that developed is perhaps shown by the fact that Ms. Graham's son by a previous marriage later changed his own surname to Du Bois, as an adult, because of his admiration for his stepfather.

While it does seem that Ms. Graham's imagination prevailed too forcefully in her book about Banneker, this should not obscure the valuable aspects of her overall work.

It is important to realize that applying the usual standards of biographical writing to the lives of black persons of the eighteenth century would leave them very little known indeed, and we would be the poorer. Blacks of Banneker's era were treated as nonpersons and produced hardly any public records or regular correspondence, while their white counterparts left mountains of records. If the words or thoughts of a black subject are limited to what can be proved beyond a doubt, the person will be silenced forever, just as his or her adversaries would have preferred. So in two cases, the ill-fated Baltimore trip (Chapter 3) and the fatal romance (Chapter 5), I have cited incidents that were based on Ms. Graham's writings—not because I believe them to be accurate in detail, but because the very fact that those tales have circulated is in itself a part of the Banneker story.

The following additional background on Ms. Graham after her second marriage is of interest, even if not highly relevant to this biography: Mr. and Mrs. Du Bois showed a partiality for the Soviet Union that caused their passports to be revoked in the 1950s, when U.S. reactions to leftist thinking were decidedly abrupt. When they finally were allowed to travel, they were given a great reception in Moscow, but then went on to visit China, which was illegal at the time. Their passports were again cancelled. Mr. Du Bois reacted adversely to these pressures, finally declaring himself officially a communist and accepting Kwame Nkrumah's invitation to spend the rest of his life in Ghana, where he held court for many visitors from America. Whether he truly espoused Marxism or was merely fighting back, it is noteworthy that Shirley Graham, before marrying him, had told an interviewer at the National Association of Colored Women in 1947 that "Communism offers no solution to the negro in his search for freedom from racial intolerance."

Bibliography

Books

Allen, William G. *Wheatley, Banneker, and Horton.* Freeport, NY: Self-published, 1970.

Appiah, Kwame, and Henry Louis Gates, Jr. *Africana Encyclopedia.* New York: Perseus Books, 1999.

Azuonye, Chukwuma. *Dogon.* New York: Rosen Publishing Group, 1998.

Banks, William M. *Black Intellectuals.* New York: W. W. Norton, 1996.

Barck, Oscar T. *Colonial America.* New York: Macmillan, 1968.

Bedini, Silvio. *Benjamin Banneker.* Rancho Cordova, CA: Landmark Enterprises, 1972.

Beyer, Steven L. *The Star Guide.* Boston: Little, Brown, 1986.

Brandt, John, and Stephen Maran. *New Horizons in Astronomy,* 2nd ed. San Francisco: W. H. Freeman & Co., 1972.

Brugger, Robert J. *Maryland—A Middle Temperament: 1634–1980.* Baltimore: Johns Hopkins University Press, 1988.

Conley, Kevin. *Benjamin Banneker: Scientist and Mathematician.* New York: Chelsea House Publishers, 1989.

Durham, Frank, and Robert D. Purrington. *Frame of the Universe.* New York: Columbia University Press, 1983.

Fermi, E. *Galileo and the Scientific Revolution.* New York: Basic Books, 1961.

Flexner, James T. *Washington: The Indispensable Man.* Boston: Little, Brown, 1969.

Foner, Philip S. *Blacks in the American Revolution.* Westport, CT: Greenwood Press, 1975.

Franklin, Joseph, and Loren Schweninger. *Runaway Slaves: Rebels on the Plantation.* New York: Oxford University Press, 1999.

Graham, Shirley. *"Your Most Humble Servant."* New York: Julian Messner, 1949.

Grégoire, Bishop Henri. *De la littérature des Negres, ou Recherches sur leur facultés intellectuelles, leurs qualités morales et leur littérature* [On the literature of blacks, or research on their intellectual abilities, their moral qualities, and their literature]. Paris: Maradan, Libraire, 1808.

Hathaway, Nancy. *The Friendly Guide to the Universe.* New York: Viking/Penguin Group, 1994.

Ley, Willy. *Watchers of the Skies.* New York: Viking Press, 1963.

Loftin, T. L. *Contest for a Capital.* Washington, D.C.: J. T. Loftin Publishers, 1989.

Lopez, Claude-Anne, and Eugenia W. Herbert. *The Private Franklin.* New York: W. W. Norton, 1975.

McCollough, David. *John Adams.* New York: Simon & Schuster, 2001.

Middlekauff, Robert. *The Glorious Cause.* New York: Oxford University Press, 1982.

Moore, Patrick. *The Guinness Book of Astronomy,* 2nd ed. Enfield, Middlesex, England: Guinness Superlatives Ltd., 1983.

Pasachoff, Jay M. *Astronomy: From the Earth to the Universe,* 3rd ed. Philadelphia: Saunders College Publishing, 1987.

Price, Fred W. *The Planet Observer's Handbook.* Cambridge: Cambridge University Press, 1994.

Quarles, Benjamin. *The Negro in the American Revolution.* Chapel Hill, N.C.: University of North Carolina Press, 1961.

Randall, Willard S. *George Washington.* New York: Henry Holt & Co., 1997.

Reiss, Oscar. *Blacks in Colonial America.* Jefferson, N.C.: McFarland, 1997.

Sobel, Dava. *Longitude.* New York: Walker & Company, 1995.

Thane, Elswyth. *Washington's Lady.* New York: Dodd, Mead, 1960.

Travers, Paul J. *The Patapsco*. Baltimore, MD: Tidewater Publishers and the Maryland Historical Society, 1990.

Tyson, Martha Ellicott. *Memoir of Benjamin Banneker*, as told to her daughter, Anne T. Kirk. Philadelphia: Philadelphia Friends Book Association, 1884.

Van Doren, Carl. *Benjamin Franklin*. New York: Viking Press, 1956.

Zaslavsky, Claudia. *Africa Counts*. New York: Prindle, Weber, and Group, 1980.

Articles and Lectures

Baker, Henry E. "The Negro Mathematician and Astronomer," *Journal of Negro History*, vol. 3 (1918), 99–118.

Buchanan, George. *An Oration Upon the Moral and Political Evil of Slavery*, at a public meeting of the Maryland Society for Promoting the Abolition of Slavery, Baltimore, MD, July 4, 1791.

Conway, Moncure Daniel. "Benjamin Banneker." *The Atlantic Monthly*, vol. 11, issue 63 (January 1863), 79–84.

Ellis, Joseph J. "Jefferson's Cop-Out." *Civilization* magazine (December 1996), 46–54.

Huckenpahler, Victoria. "George Washington Dances." *Dance* magazine, July 1976.

Hurry, Robert J. "Benjamin Banneker's Home." *Maryland Historical Magazine*, vol. 84, no. 4 (1989), 42–47.

Latrobe, John H. B. Lecture to the Maryland Historical Society, 1844. (Also published in *Maryland Colonization Journal*, May 1845, 68–73).

Norris, J. Saurin. Lecture (from posthumous papers of Martha E. Tyson) before the Maryland Historical Society, 1854.

Simmons, Melody. "Banneker Museum Takes Root" (Banneker Park, Oella, MD, color layout), *Baltimore Sun*, February 1, 1995, p. BI.

Index

CPSIA information can be obtained
at www.ICGtesting.com
Printed in the USA
BVOW06*1133100517

483731BV00016B/562/P